UNITED PURSUIT

Virginia's Journey to the 2019 National Championship

Cover and book design: Josh Crutchmer

Photos courtesy of: Matt Riley/UVA athletic department, AP Images, Atlantis Paradise Island
Facing page: Photo by Matt Riley

ISBN: 978-1-940056-77-7
KCI Sports Publishing 3340 Whiting Avenue, Suite 5 Stevens Point, WI 54481
Phone: 1-800-697-3756 Fax: 715-344-2668
www.kcisports.com

This book is officially licensed and endorsed by the University of Virginia.

*The Publisher would like to thank the University of Virginia athletic department,
Todd Goodale, Erich Bacher, Jim Daves, Jeff White and Matt Riley for their assistance
in the production of this book.*

Printed in the United States of America

From Five Pillars to Top of the Basketball World

The University of Virginia Basketball family is headed by head coach Tony Bennett, and before you are even a part of it, you understand that this family is defined by five pillars: humility, passion, unity, servanthood and thankfulness.

Coach Bennett's uncompromised vision for this program laid the groundwork for an NCAA title that took a decade to achieve. Fans of the program have come to love Coach Bennett's system of Pack Line defense. Those who aren't fans called us boring, and they didn't Embrace the Pace. But as of April 8, 2019, when we beat Texas Tech in the NCAA championship game, everyone has to respect it.

Most collegiate basketball seasons end with a loss. It's painful in the moment. The players and coaches dedicated countless hours to that season, and they feel the disappointment of falling short of a conference championship or national title. Just one year before achieving the most difficult task in collegiate sports, many of the same UVA players and coaches saw the season end with a historic loss to UMBC in the first round of the 2018 NCAA Tournament. It was devastating to witness.

But life works in mysterious ways. I believe that experiencing that low is what brought this team to the incredible height of this season. It was a pleasure to watch those guys work through that adversity and come out on top knowing that my fellow basketball alums and I were there for them every step of the way.

I am beyond proud of what they have achieved this season and what these guys will go on to achieve in the future.

Celebrate this season Virginia fans, and save this book to revisit the Cavaliers' magical moments and unforgettable team that rewarded your faith in them with a national championship.

Go 'Hoos!

— **Malcolm Brogdon**
Virginia Two-time All-American
2017 NBA Rookie of the Year, Milwaukee Bucks
BA – History, 2015
MPP – Public Policy, 2016

Malcolm Brogdon — currently a star in the NBA for the Milwaukee Bucks and the 2017 Rookie of the Year — was the 2016 ACC Player of the Year and Defensive Player of the Year for the Cavaliers under coach Tony Bennett.

Matt Riley

Contents

The **2018-19 Cavaliers**, after a closed practice at the Final Four.

Matt Riley

against Texas Tech, and the Cavaliers are national champions.

Associated Press

Before a Championship, a Reckoning With the Past

By now everyone knows the story.

After sweeping the ACC's regular-season and tournament titles, and posting a school-record 31 victories, UVA entered last season's NCAA tourney as the No. 1 overall seed. The Cavaliers aimed to make history by winning the first NCAA title in program history.

Instead, Virginia made history of a different sort, becoming the first No. 1 seed to lose to a No. 16 seed, falling to little-known University of Maryland-Baltimore County in a first-round game at the Spectrum Center in Charlotte.

The loss was as tough as they come. For Bennett. For his players. For Virginia fans everywhere.

For days … weeks … months … whenever Virginia was mentioned in basketball circles, the topic would inevitably turn to how a #1 could lose to a #16.

As the Cavaliers entered the 2018-19 season, Bennett knew questions about the loss to UMBC were coming.

"I think it's a mistake if you just say, 'Well, it happened, it was a fluke' and sweep it under the rug and not deal with it," Bennett told reporters at ACC Operation Basketball. "Just the fact that it happened, it's part of our story. We've owned that and will continue to own it. You have to embrace it. That's not going to change."

"I made my peace with it. I can't change what happened," Bennett continued. But the loss "kind of sparked something in me," he said.

"I desperately want Virginia and this team that I coach to have a chance to hopefully one day go to a Final Four, play for a national championship, win a national championship," Bennett said. "I want to really go at this in the right way. [The setback] has inspired me in a way that maybe only a loss like that can. But it did something else that I think is as important or more important: It made me realize if that doesn't happen, I'm still OK. It was unbelievable to win like we won, and it was joyful. But it wasn't the end-all, be-all. And it was really painful to lose like we did – really painful, humbling – but it wasn't the end-all, be-all."

To their credit, Bennett and his players never ducked the loss. They discussed the defeat – and their resolve to learn from the experience -- during team meetings at John Paul Jones Arena. Then, together, they regrouped, attacking offseason workouts with a passion and a new rallying cry: ∞∞∞

In 2018, there was nothing Kyle Guy (5) could do other than console teammates after top-seeded Virginia lost to 16th-seeded Maryland-Baltimore County in the NCAA Tournament.

Matt Riley

'I think it's a mistake if you just say, 'Well, it happened, it was a fluke' and sweep it under the rug and not deal with it. Just the fact that it happened, it's part of our story. We've owned that and will continue to own it. You have to embrace it. That's not going to change.'

Head coach Tony Bennett, at ACC Operation Basketball, on the NCAA Tournament loss to UMBC the previous season

United Pursuit

"So many people say, 'You've got to get back, you've got to vindicate yourself or validate what happened,' " Bennett said. "This is about us running to the starting line of the season and taking it as far as we can possibly go. It's about growing from last year's unbelievable success, to growing from last year's very humbling loss, and using it to help us respond and be better. These guys, we're united in what we're pursuing. That's one of the things we're talking about is being united in our pursuit and going after it."

Did they ever go after it. From the early-season Battle 4 Atlantis championship, to the ACC regular-season title, a school-record 35 wins, a and the greatest NCAA tournament run a 'Hoos fan could ever ask for.

Long-suffering Virginia fans have waited patiently for this type of season.

From Wally Walker leading the Cavaliers to their first NCAA tournament appearance in 1976, to Terry Holland and Ralph Sampson breaking down the Final Four door in the early 1980's, to the Cinderella run in 1984 when the 'Hoos came within an eyelash of knocking off the eventual national champion Houston Cougars. So many years, UVA came so close but could never quite break through.

Finally, the wait is over.

But it was how this team won that made the championship run so memorable. Virginia's 2019 tournament wins were infused with a flair for the dramatic. Down 14 to Gardner-Webb in round one, they refused to hear the whispers of another collapse, vanquishing the ghost of tournaments past with that first win. Fighting off tough Oklahoma and Oregon teams to advance to the Elite Eight. Trading blows with a physical Purdue squad, it took "The Shot" by Mamadi Diakite to send the game to overtime, where UVA refused to be denied its trip to the Final Four. The roller coaster of a semifinal, with Kyle Guy drilling three pressure-packed free throws with six-tenths of a second left to defeat Auburn. And in a final act, De'Andre Hunter leading the charge in one of the most entertaining national championship games in recent history.

As exciting—and to be fair, nerve-wracking—as their play was on the court, these Cavaliers conveyed the opposite tone off it. Patient. Steady. Focused. United in their pursuit.

In a word — champions.

One of the many team-building outings the Hoos took prior to the 2018-19 season was whitewater rafting as a group.

Whitewater Photography (used by permission)

Before getting serious about chasing a national championship, the Cavaliers were loose and having fun during their preseason photo shoot.

Matt Riley

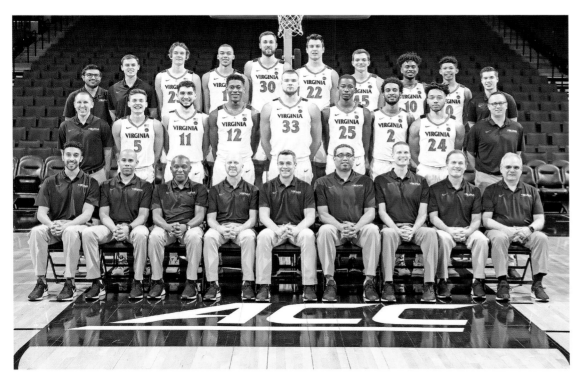

Preseason media day and team photo at John Paul Jones Arena.

Matt Riley

'Hoos Open Season in Style

By Jeff White

November 6, 2018

CHARLOTTESVILLE — In his University of Virginia debut, point guard Kihei Clark wasted no time establishing himself as a fan favorite at John Paul Jones Arena.

A minute after entering the game, the 5-9 freshman from Los Angeles hit a floater that delighted the crowd of 13,807. Later in the first half, Clark collected assists on back-to-back 3-pointers, the first by junior guard Ty Jerome and the second by junior forward Braxton Key.

When Clark left the game for the last time Tuesday night, with 2:35 remaining, UVA fans saluted him with a warm ovation, and their enthusiasm was understandable.

In his 24-plus minutes off the bench, Clark totaled a game-high six assists to help the fifth-ranked Cavaliers pull away for a 73-42 victory over the Tigers.

"I don't know how to describe it," Clark said. "It was crazy. It was a great atmosphere. I loved it."

He focused, Clark said, on "being a pass-first point guard and looking to get my guys involved. When you've got people around you like Kyle Guy and Ty Jerome shooting the ball like that, it makes my job easy."

Guy, a 6-2 junior who was a third-team All-American last season, was uncharacteristically cold Tuesday, making only 1 of 5 shots from 3-point range. But Jerome, a 6-5 junior, was 6 for 9 from beyond the arc and led all scorers with 20 points.

"He just has that innate feel of when to kind of seize the game," Towson head coach Pat Skerry said.

Jerome made the All-ACC third team in 2017-18, when he was the Cavaliers' primary ballhandler and helped them sweep the conference's regular-season and tournament titles. With the arrival of Clark, Virginia can use Jerome, who has almost unlimited shooting range, off the ball more.

"He's super quick, and I think what separates him is he really has a great feel for the game, too," Jerome said of Clark. "So when you mix those two things together, he really can control the game. He'll be a really big piece for us this year."

The opener also marked the UVA debut of the 6-8, 225-pound Key, a transfer from Alabama whom the NCAA granted immediate eligibility this season. He contributed seven points, nine rebounds, one assists, one steal and one blocked shot in 29 minutes.

Head coach Tony Bennett, whose parents attended the game, started Key, Guy, Jerome, 6-10 fifth-year senior Jack Salt and 6-7 redshirt sophomore De'Andre Hunter. Salt played only 14 minutes and 47 seconds, much less than UVA's other starters in a game in which Bennett often opted to use smaller lineups.

"This is a mobile team with some size, and I haven't had that, and I think that's a strength of ours," said Bennett, who's in his 10th season at Virginia. "I like the versatility of this team."

Hunter, the ACC's Sixth Man of the Year in 2017-18, suffered a season-ending injury in the ACC tournament and missed Virginia's first-round game in the NCAA tourney, a stunning loss to UMBC.

Against Towson, he scored 13 points and grabbed a game-high 10 rebounds.

"Just being back out there with the team, it was really fun," Hunter said.

"Me and Braxton, we play really well together. He's very versatile, and when we're on the court I feel like we do good things for our defense."

Previous page: Forward Jay Huff dunks during Virginia's 73-42 win over Towson in the season opener.

Right: Cavaliers players take the court for pregame introductions and the UVA cheerleaders look on during the season opener.

Matt Riley

19

Clark Ready to Apply Pressure

By Jeff White

CHARLOTTESVILLE — As a senior last season at Taft Charter High in Los Angeles, point guard Kihei Clark shot 41 percent from 3-point range, made 81 percent of his free throws, and averaged 19.4 points and 7.2 assists per game.

At the University of Virginia, Clark has flashed those offensive skills in practices and in scrimmages against Richmond and Villanova. But what's really endeared him to head coach Tony Bennett is Clark's defensive tenacity.

"He's a pest," Bennett said. "He gets after the ball. He's quick and he's strong, though he's smaller. But his on-ball defense [is outstanding]. I haven't coached a lot of guys like him that can really pick up [anywhere on the court]."

At a UVA practice over the summer, junior guard Ty Jerome grew so annoyed by Clark's pressure that he threw the basketball at the 5-9, 155-pound freshman's head.

"That means he got under Ty's skin, so he was doing his job," said Bennett, who laughed as he recounted the story early this semester.

Reminded last week of that episode, UVA guard Kyle Guy couldn't resist a jab at his close friend and classmate.

"I didn't know Ty was so mentally weak, and you can tell him I said that," Guy said, smiling.

Guy continued in a more serious vein. "Actually, that's what Kihei brings, and that's going to be big for us. He'll pick up full-court, and he's really going to bother a lot of people and

get some [deflections]. He's been a problem in practice defensively, and I think he's really going to help us."

So does Jerome. "He'll definitely add a lot to our defense and our offense," Jerome said. "His energy doing whatever his role is this year will be tremendous for us."

Virginia's trademark Pack Line defense has stymied countless opponents during Bennett's tenure. Most recently, the Wahoos led the nation in scoring defense last season. Rarely, though, has Bennett had an on-the-ball defender as dogged as Clark.

Jontel Evans excelled in that role on Bennett's first four teams at Virginia, and graduate transfer Nigel Johnson had some good moments last season.

"They're all a little bit different," Bennett said, "but [each has] that kind of tenacity and ability to pester the ball and ignite the guys behind them. On-ball, [Clark is] willing and aggressive and talented in that regard, and he's getting better off the ball."

As a guard with the NBA's Charlotte Hornets, Bennett recalled, he had to battle 5-3 Muggsy Bogues in practice, "so I know that someone who's up under you and always doing that can be a problem."

The Pack Line can be effective even if the perimeter players aren't outstanding defenders individually. But having a guard such as Clark who "can apply pressure or heat or activity on the ball," Bennett said, makes the defense that much tougher.

"We always liken it to a quarterback in the pocket," Bennett said.

"If he can window-shop and has time, he'll be able to dissect and pick apart a defense. But if he's rushed a little bit or feels pressure, it changes everything, and that's a big part of it for all of our guys."

When he's able to force the opposing point guard to pass the ball in the backcourt, Clark said, "that's a great feeling for me, just knowing I could disrupt their offense early on."

Clark, whose father, Malik, played basketball at the University of Hawaii at Hilo, arrived at UVA in June and began the process of adjusting to the college game.

"I think I've definitely grown," Clark said, "just learning the offense and being able to pick when to shoot and when to pass."

His hometown of Woodland Hills, Calif., is nearly 2,600 miles from Charlottesville, but that didn't faze Clark. Like another point guard from L.A., London Perrantes, who was a four-year starter at Virginia, Clark couldn't pass up the opportunity to play for Bennett and test himself in the ACC.

"It's a long way from home, but basketball is what I wanted to do," said Clark. "My family and I knew that distance wasn't going to matter."

Right: Kihei Clark on the court during the Hoos' opener against Towson.

Matt Riley

One Trophy Down, A Lot More to Play For

By Jeff White

November 21-23, 2018

NASSAU, BAHAMAS — Fourth-ranked UVA headed home to Charlottesville with an unbeaten record and a well-earned trophy after capturing the Battle 4 Atlantis tournament.

Playing three games in three days, the Cavaliers defeated Middle Tennessee 74-52, Dayton 66-59, and, in the championship game, 25th-ranked Wisconsin 53-46.

This marked the sixth straight championship for Virginia in a Thanksgiving holiday tournament. In addition to UVA, Middle Tennessee, Dayton and Wisconson, the field included Florida, Oklahoma, Butler and Stanford.

"We weren't pushed early [in the season]," UVA head coach Tony Bennett said, "and so to be in some games like this was very important. Like the ACC tournament, if you're fortunate enough to advance, three games in that amount of time, it tests your mettle. It was a test of our system, and it really was a test individually of what our guys had in their mind and in their heart. We talked about refusing to yield."

With the win over previously unbeaten Wisconsin, a school to which Bennett has strong ties, the Cavaliers improved to 6-0. Virginia led by 10 points with 6:19 to play, only to have the Bad-gers cut their deficit to five on three occasions.

Down the stretch, though, the Wahoos made enough plays late to secure the victory – and the championship trophy.

"It was just sort of a slugfest at the end," Bennett said, "and I'm glad we were the last man standing."

Redshirt sophomore De'Andre Hunter, a 6-7 forward from Philadelphia, was named the tournament's MVP after averaging 19.3 points, 7.7 rebounds and 3.3 assists per game.

"He's taken his foot off the brake, as we like to say, and we need that," Bennett said.

Hunter, the ACC's Sixth Man of the Year in 2017-18, shot 61.8 percent from the floor and 81.3 percent from the line in the Bahamas.

"I get equally excited about what he's doing defensively," Bennett said.

The Cavaliers encountered little resistance in their tournament opener against Middle Tennessee, a game in which Hunter and junior guard Kyle Guy scored 15 points apiece and junior forward Braxton added 13 points and seven rebounds.

Against Dayton, however, UVA fell behind early before ral-lying to take a 27-22 halftime lead. The Cavaliers were unable to pull away in the second half, but Hunter, junior guard Ty Je-rome and freshman guard Kihei Clark helped them hold off the Flyers.

Hunter finished with a season-high 23 points. Jerome scored all 15 of his points after intermission, and the 5-9 Clark contributed nine points off the bench, then his season high.

The championship game marked the second meeting be-tween UVA and Wisconsin in less than a year. On Nov. 27, 2017, in the Big Ten/ACC Challenge, the Cavaliers had de-feated the Badgers 49-37 at John Paul Jones Arena.

The rematch featured many of the same players, including Ethan Happ, Wisconsin's standout center. Happ finished with 22 points, 15 rebounds, six assists and four blocks against UVA in the Bahamas, but he also had six turnovers in the face of Jack Salt's aggressive defense.

Salt, a 6-10 fifth-year senior, pulled down five rebounds in the championship game. Hunter led the Cavaliers with 20 points and nine boards, and Clark chipped in five points, five rebounds, three steals and two assists in his first college start.

Left top: Braxton Key puts up a shot against Middle Tennessee in the Cavaliers' first game in the Battle 4 Atlantis tournament.

Left bottom: Mamadi Diakite drives to the basket guarded by Wisconsin forward Ethan Happ in the championship game.

Right: The 'Hoos celebrate winning the Bad Boy Mowers Battle 4 Atlantis in Nassau, Bahamas.

Photos courtesy of Atlantis Paradise Island

Diakite Growing On and Off Court

By Jeff White

CHARLOTTESVILLE — When he arrived in the United States in January 2014 and enrolled at Blue Ridge School, Mamadi Diakite spoke four languages fluently.

English was not one of them. Would he have thought then that, several years later, he'd be standing in front of a class and delivering a speech at the University of Virginia?

"Never in English," Diakite said.

But that's what he's done this semester in Speaking in Public, a course taught by Denise Stewart in UVA's drama department. Diakite, a native of Guinea, is in his fourth year of college, and much has changed since he arrived at the University in the summer of 2015.

"He's just grown so much," said T.J. Grams, the academic advisor for the men's basketball team. "He likes learning. He enjoys his classes. He's really built a lot of good relationships on Grounds with faculty members and tutors. His greatest strength as a student is his personality. People love him, he is always willing to engage in class."

Diakite is majoring in French, with a minor in Global Culture and Commerce. He's now fluent in English, as well as in French, Malinke, Soussou and Peul, the languages he mastered before coming to America.

The 6-9, 230-pound redshirt junior is more comfortable in head coach Tony Bennett's program, too.

"It does feel different," Diakite said after starting 22 of 38 games for the national champions.

"When I came in, I knew nothing," said Diakite, who weighed 190 pounds when he enrolled at UVA. "When I say I knew nothing, I'm relating it to the language. I'm also relating it to communication. It was hard for me to communicate. Right now, everything has gotten easier. I'm able to understand everyone, it's clear, but I've still got to do a good job of bringing myself to the next level, because that's what the team needs."

When he left Guinea, Diakite recalled, "I didn't know anything about America, really. I was mostly focused on Europe."

The learning process began in earnest at Blue Ridge, a private school about 20 miles north of Charlottesville, and has continued at UVA.

"He's just become a lot more independent," Grams said. "It took him a long time to understand there's a language barrier to get over, but also a cultural expectation, too. What it meant to show up on time, and the understanding that you're supposed to be sitting in a classroom five minutes before it starts. He's really embraced that, I think."

The magnitude of Diakite's learning curve at times has tested the patience of basketball staffers, but his growth is a testament "to our culture and to Coach Bennett and how supportive he's been of Mamadi's experience," Grams said.

In 2015-16, when Diakite was redshirting, Bennett allowed him to miss practice every Wednesday in order to attend a not-for-credit ESL (English as a Second Language) course.

"Coach really took the long view of him developmentally," Grams said. "Not just on the floor, but off."

On the court, this was a pivotal year for Diakite, a key reserve for the Wahoos the past two seasons. "He's always shown glimpses, but it's been in short spurts," associate head coach Jason Williford said. "He was able to put those spurts together for a longer time and was able to do that consistently."

As a redshirt freshman in 2016-17, Diakite averaged 3.8 points per game. He was more productive last season, averaging 5.4 points, and had several memorable performances. But he says he was "a little laid-back" for the first half of the season.

"This year I realized, wow, I'm in a big situation now," Diakite said. "I needed to take care of all of my stuff, on and off the court. I didn't have any room for mistakes."

He knows that it's not enough to be in shape. Mental toughness is required to thrive in Bennett's system.

"I think he's shown that in the offseason," Williford said. "He worked extremely hard on his game, and he's gotten older and wiser. I expect big things from Mamadi. I've seen the work he's put in. I work with the bigs, so I am all in his corner. I want him to continue to give us a big punch."

Right: Mamadi Diakite controls the ball against George Washington.

Matt Riley

'Hoos Make Themselves at Home in College Park

By Jeff White

COLLEGE PARK, MD. — Maryland fans raised the chant before the game, when an upset was still a possibility, and again in the final seconds, when all hope was gone and they had nothing to cheer:

"UMBC! UMBC!"

"We knew that that was going to happen," Virginia redshirt sophomore De'Andre Hunter said Wednesday night at Maryland's Xfinity Center. "We were prepared for it."

Hunter smiled. "If they want to chant another team's name while we're winning, I guess that's the best they can do."

UVA's historic 2017-18 season ended, as anyone who follows college basketball knows, with a shocking loss to No. 16 seed UMBC in the NCAA tournament's first round. But this is a new season. The Cavaliers again rank among the nation's elite, as they showed Wednesday night in their first road test of the season.

In a nationally televised ACC/Big Ten Challenge game, No. 4 Virginia defeated No. 24 Maryland 76-71 before a sellout crowd of 17,950. Five players scored in double figures for UVA (7-0), including fifth-year senior Jack Salt, who finished with a career-high 12 points.

The win was the Wahoos' eighth in their past nine meetings with the Terrapins.

"We lost to a great team tonight that played at a high level," Maryland head coach Mark Turgeon said.

These schools no longer play each other in basketball twice every season, as they did when Maryland was a member of the ACC. This was their first meeting since Dec. 3, 2014, in fact, and UVA's players aren't especially well-versed in the rivalry.

Even so, they could tell during warmups that this was not a typical non-conference game. The Terrapins made it a "blackout" for which students dressed accordingly.

"It's a great atmosphere," Virginia freshman point guard Kihei Clark said. "If you're a basketball player, I don't know how you can't love something like that."

The Cavaliers, who went into halftime ahead by nine, stretched their lead to 48-31 on a Salt tip-in with 16:42 to play. The Terrapins (6-1), unfazed by Virginia's Pack Line defense, battled back and twice cut their deficit to four in the final 4:30.

But each time Virginia responded: first with a Salt follow dunk that made it 63-57, and then with a Ty Jerome 3-pointer that made it 66-59 with 2:48 left.

"We do a really good job of never really worrying or wavering from our ways," junior guard Kyle Guy said, "so there was never any panic or anything like that. We just knew what we had to do to pull away a little bit more."

Guy was 5 for 9 from beyond the arc and led all scorers with 18 points. Jerome, a 6-5 junior guard, added 17 points. The 6-7 Hunter had 15 points, five rebounds and four assists, and 6-8 junior Braxton Key, a transfer from Alabama, contributed 10 points and two steals off the bench.

And then there was the 6-10, 250-pound Salt, who came in with modest averages of 3.0 points and 3.8 rebounds per game.

Matched against 6-10, 240-pound sophomore Bruno Fernardo, who's projected to be a first-round NBA draft pick, Salt totaled 12 points, seven rebounds, one assist, one blocked shot, and one steal Wednesday night. He was 6 for 7 from the floor, with four dunks.

"I'm just so happy for him," Guy said. "We were joking [before the game] about how his career high is only 10 and he hasn't dunked at all this year, and he put us all to bed tonight."

Fernando finished with 14 points, 11 rebounds and two blocks and wowed the crowd with his athleticism. But his eagerness to challenge shooters in the lane created opportunities for Salt, who's known more for his bone-rattling screens than his scoring.

"Bruno's such a good shot-blocker," Virginia head coach Tony Bennett said. "He's so athletic, and he goes after stuff. So when shot-blockers go after it, if you can get it on the rim, there's going to be open lanes or alleys to the glass, and Jack was all over there."

For the game, Maryland shot 54 percent from the floor, a statistic that didn't thrill Bennett. But he loved his team's ball security. UVA tied the program record for fewest turnovers in a game (two). Each came on an offensive foul.

"We took care of the ball," Bennett said. "I don't want to minimize that, because [the Terps] can get out and run. And our ability to only have two turnovers and not give them any loose-ball or live-ball turnovers, I think, was a big storyline."

Right: Ty Jerome launches a three over Maryland's Anthony Cowan Jr.

Matt Riley

Clark's Grit Sparks Cavaliers

By Jeff White

December 9, 2018

CHARLOTTESVILLE — Muggsy Bogues' long NBA career ended when Kihei Clark was still an infant, so they're of different generations. But Clark has access to YouTube, and he knows that when Tony Bennett compares him to Bogues – as Virginia's head men's basketball coach likes to do – it's praise of the highest order.

Bennett, who played with Bogues for three seasons on the Charlotte Hornets, still lights up when talking about his former teammate's suffocating on-ball defense.

"It means a lot," the 5-9 Clark said of being likened to the 5-3 Bogues. "He's a smaller guard, and he played basketball at the highest level. I try to play defense like him and have the heart like he did."

On a snowy afternoon in Central Virginia, Clark's grit was on full display at John Paul Jones Arena.

He's scheduled to have surgery Monday to repair a hairline fracture in his left wrist. That didn't keep him from playing Sunday against VCU with a cast covering his wrist and much of his left hand.

"It didn't affect his heart or his legs, that's for sure," Bennett said.

A freshman from the Woodland Hills section of Los Angeles, Clark finished with nine points, a game-high four assists,

two rebounds and two steals in the fourth-ranked Cavaliers' 57-49 victory over the Rams.

What delighted Bennett most, however, was Clark's relentless defense, especially the 10-second violation he forced VCU guard P.J. Byrd into at the 5:25 mark of the second half. As the home fans roared their appreciation, Bennett bounded onto the court and slapped hands with Clark.

"This was the most amped I've ever seen [Bennett]," junior guard Ty Jerome said.

Bennett said Clark "about made me jump out of my shoes when he got that 10-second call."

Clark's defensive gem came during the 15-2 run with which Virginia (9-0) seized control of this fiercely contested non-conference game.

With 6:30 left, the Rams led 43-38, but back-to-back baskets by Jerome – the second a 3-pointer from NBA range – tied the game. Then Clark forced the 10-second violation, after which fifth-year senior center Jack Salt made 1 of 2 free throws to put the Wahoos up 44-43.

VCU (7-3) briefly regained the lead, at 45-44, but UVA answered with a five-point possession on which junior guard Kyle Guy was fouled away from the ball while Jerome buried a trey.

Guy sank both ends of a one-and-one, and suddenly the

'Hoos were up four.

"UVA beat us today, and they beat us down the stretch, and that's the sign of a good team," VCU head coach Mike Rhoades said.

The Cavaliers' lead was six when, with 2:35 left, Clark forced another turnover, tying up 6-2 guard Marcus Evans on a drive.

The possession arrow pointed Virginia's way, and redshirt sophomore De'Andre Hunter capped the next possession with two free throws.

Clark played 32 minutes and 45 seconds, and he spent much of that time guarding Evans, who came in as VCU's leading scorer. Evans hit only 1 of 10 shots from the floor Sunday, and he turned the ball over three times.

"I just wanted to keep him in front, try to disrupt their offense as much as possible, and apply ball pressure," said Clark, who injured his wrist while taking a charge last Monday night in UVA's win over Morgan State at JPJ.

"It was not the prettiest shooting game," Bennett said, "but I don't think you can fault the defensive effort and some of the plays that were made."

Right: Kihei Clark passes for one of his game-high four assists against VCU.

Matt Riley

'Hoos Score 100, Bennett Wins 300th

By Jeff White

December 31, 2018

CHARLOTTESVILLE — On New Year's Eve, the holiday crowd at John Paul Jones Arena saved its most frenzied celebration for the final play.

That was not because walk-on guard Grant Kersey's 3-pointer lifted the home team to victory – the outcome of this non-conference game had long since been settled – but because his trey pushed the University of Virginia men's basketball team to triple figures for the first time in its 10 seasons under head coach Tony Bennett.

With fourth-ranked UVA leading Marshall by 33 points and the shot clock off Monday afternoon, Bennett would have preferred for his team to have held the ball on the game's final possession. But with the Thundering Herd applying pressure defense, Jayden Nixon crossed midcourt and passed the ball to Kersey, who spotted his former Albemarle High School teammate Austin Katstra open in the left corner.

Katstra's 3-point attempt missed, but Kersey, who doubles as one of the Cavaliers' managers, grabbed the long rebound and launched an off-balance shot from beyond the arc.

It dropped through, naturally, and pandemonium ensued at JPJ. In the stands, jubilant fans roared their approval. On the court, Kersey's teammates mobbed him.

"We wanted him to shoot it," said junior guard Kyle Guy, who lives with Kersey.

For the Wahoos, their 100-64 victory over Marshall, which advanced to the NCAA tournament's second round last season, capped the non-conference portion of their schedule. The 'Hoos dominated almost from the opening tip. Four players scored in double figures for UVA (12-0), led by Guy, who was virtually unstoppable.

In front of a sellout crowd that included incoming recruit Kadin Shedrick, a 6-10 post player from Raleigh, N.C., Guy hit 7 of 9 shots from 3-point range and 10 of 14 overall. His 30 points were a career high, as were his seven treys and his eight rebounds.

Guy had no complaints afterward. Still, he admitted he would not have minded posting the first double-double of his UVA career.

"I tried so hard when I went back in [in the second half] to get two more, but they weren't bouncing my way," he said, smiling. Bennett has coached several other exceptional shooters, including Klay Thompson and Joe Harris, and said Guy shares some qualities with them.

"If he's not squared up, he can kind of shift in the air and turn and then knock it in," Bennett said.

Guy "has beautiful form," Bennett said. "I think it's great how it's textbook [in the way] it comes out, and we work hard on how quick he can get his feet set and how quick he can shoot it, trying to be square. But he has that innate ability when he's not square where he can turn and, boom, get it off. I think that's a separator."

A third-team All-American in 2017-18, Guy wasn't the only Cavalier to torch the Thundering Herd (7-6).

For the game, Virginia shot 53.2 percent from the floor and held Marshall, which came to JPJ averaging 82.2 points per game, to 35.1-percent accuracy. Led by redshirt sophomore De'Andre Hunter, a long-armed 6-7 swingman, the Cavaliers forced the Herd's leading scorer, guard Jon Elmore, into a subpar performance.

Elmore, a 6-3 senior who came in averaging 19.6 points per game, missed 14 of 17 shots from the floor, including 7 of 8 from beyond the arc. He finished with a team-high 14 points, but 12 came after the 'Hoos built a 50-25 halftime lead.

Right: Grant Kersey celebrates his three-pointer against Marshall.

Matt Riley

"Dre is a fantastic defender," Guy said, "and his length bothered [Elmore]."

For Bennett, the victory was his 231st with the Cavaliers and 300th as a head coach. (He was 69-33 in three seasons at Washington State.)

Asked about his feat, Bennett said, "I'm thankful ... It just means you've had really good players. It means I've been coaching for a while. I've had a great staff. My whole hope is that in my 300 wins I've honored and respected the game, the people who've poured into my life and what I value as important, and then in the many games that I've lost, I've done the same. And that's all I can ask for, so I'm very grateful to have been given this opportunity."

GEICO

Kyle Guy celebrates from the scorer's table in the 100-64 win over Marshall.

Matt Riley

Cavaliers Make Statement in ACC Opener

By Jeff White

January 5, 2019

CHARLOTTESVILLE — Most of the fans who packed John Paul Jones Arena were in their seats well before the opening tip Saturday afternoon, and there was a noticeable buzz when the fourth-ranked Virginia men's basketball team took the floor for its ACC opener.

"The home crowd came out right," UVA head coach Tony Bennett said, and so did his team.

Against ninth-ranked Florida State, the unbeaten Cavaliers led 42-23 at the break, thanks to a tour de force by junior guard Kyle Guy, who scored 18 of his game-high 21 points in the first half. Virginia's lead grew to 29 points before FSU, pressing full-court, rallied in the final 2:35 against a lineup composed of reserves and walk-ons for a 65-52 final score.

The Seminoles scored the game's last 16 points but didn't come close to catching UVA, which won 65-52 at sold-out JPJ.

"It was awesome today," said junior guard Ty Jerome, who had a game-high six assists for Virginia (13-0 overall, 1-0 ACC). "The students are on break, but it was an amazing atmosphere."

This is the Wahoos' 10th season under Bennett, who improved his record in ACC openers to 10-0. His teams are renowned for their rugged man-to-man defense, and the Cavaliers' performance against FSU (12-2, 0-1) only enhanced that reputation. Even with their late surge, the 'Noles shot only 34.1 percent from the floor. With 2:35 remaining, they had 34 points. They came in averaging 81.3 per game.

"We were locked in and we were ready to play defensively,"

Bennett said. "Did they miss some shots? Yes. Were we perfect? No. But we said, 'We're going to work,' and at halftime I said, 'If you can, win this with your defense.'

"Offense, we've talked about many times, can come and go, but defensively you just have to make them shoot a contested shot and earn their shots and not give them second-chance points, and I thought we did that at a very acceptable level for us."

The 'Hoos, who lead the nation in scoring defense, forced two shot-clock violations, to the delight of the home fans.

"Shots come and go," Jerome said, "but when we're locked in defensively, we're really tough to beat."

FSU, which has faced such opponents as Florida, Villanova, Purdue and Connecticut this season, can attest to that.

"This is the best team we've played," head coach Leonard Hamilton said of the Cavaliers. "It's not even close. This team, with the system that they have, they're going to be very difficult to beat."

Guy broke the game open with back-to-back 3-pointers in the final two minutes of the first half. On the opening possession of the second half, he hit another trey, his school-record 11th straight over a span of two games.

"Like I always say, it's just my teammates having confidence in me and me having confidence in myself," Guy said. "When you hit a couple in a row, Coach starts to run a couple plays for you, so that really helped."

In a Dec. 31 rout of Marshall at JPJ, Guy made his final six shots from beyond the arc and finished with a career-best 30

points. He made his first five 3-pointers against FSU, an exhibition of marksmanship that Bennett called "a clinic."

Hamilton said FSU's coaches, studying Guy on videotape, have commented that they "don't even know if he's looking at the goal. Especially on some of those out-of-bounds plays, he'll just catch it and turn around in the air and knock it in."

That Guy was capable of putting up big numbers was no surprise for the 'Noles. What they didn't expect was the offensive brilliance of UVA reserve Braxton Key, a transfer from Alabama who came in averaging 6.3 points per game. Against FSU, the 6-8, 225-pound junior scored 20 points – by far his most as a Cavalier – and grabbed six rebounds. Key made 7 of 11 shots from the floor, including 2 of 5 from 3-point range.

"It felt great," Key said. "My teammates had confidence in me and I had confidence in myself. Whenever I had an open look, I just tried to be a little more aggressive today than normal, and shots were falling for me today."

At the offensive end, Bennett said, Key "really let the game come, took the open shots when they were there and attacked when it was there. That's his game.

"He's kind of a complete player who does a little bit of everything and understands how to play. I was as pleased with his defense as his offense."

Right: Kyle Guy drives against Florida State. Guy scored 21 in the game.

Matt Riley

The Cavaliers line up before their ACC opener against Florida State.

Matt Riley

37

'Hoos Humble Hokies at JPJ

By Jeff White

January 15, 2019

CHARLOTTESVILLE — The box score in front of him confirmed what University of Virginia head coach Tony Bennett had witnessed over the previous two hours: another dominant performance by his basketball team, which dismantled a top-10 opponent at John Paul Jones Arena for the second time in two weeks.

Against one of the ACC's top defenses, Virginia shot 54.2 percent from 3-point range and 58.5 percent overall Tuesday night. The Cavaliers collected assists on 18 of their 31 field goals, held a prolific offense well under its shooting and scoring averages, and won the rebounding battle 27-19.

"This was a great team effort," Bennett said after fourth-ranked UVA took sole possession of first place in the ACC with an 81-59 win over ninth-ranked Virginia Tech.

In almost every category, the Cavaliers (16-0 overall, 4-0 ACC) bested the Hokies (14-2, 3-1). Every one of UVA's rotation players had a positive impact in the first of these rivals' two Commonwealth Clash meetings: from Ty Jerome to De'Andre Hunter to Kyle Guy to Jack Salt to Mamadi Diakite to Braxton Key to Kihei Clark to Jay Huff.

"You can tell they have fun playing together, and how could you not in this environment?" Bennett said.

Indeed, the sellout crowd of 14,623, which included such former UVA players as Isaiah Wilkins, Ralph Sampson, Richard Morgan, Mamadi Diane and Tunji Soroye, was in full voice throughout.

"The crowd was amazing tonight," Guy said.

That's usually the case at JPJ, and Bennett knew the fans would provide an emotional lift to his team. Still, he reminded his players that execution would be the key to defeating the Hokies, who rallied in overtime last season to stun the Cavaliers at JPJ.

Emotion "really wasn't going to matter," Bennett said. "That can get you by for maybe a minute or two, and then it comes down to, do you do well what matters most?"

As the Wahoos had Jan. 5 in a one-sided win over then-No. 9 Florida State at JPJ, they controlled the game from the start Tuesday night. Jerome led the way.

The 6-5 junior had a hand in each of UVA's first 19 points. Jerome assisted on two Diakite baskets (a layup and a dunk) and on 3-pointers by Hunter and Huff. No. 11 scored the other nine points himself.

Jerome finished with 14 points and a career-high 12 assists, the most any player has had at JPJ, which opened in 2006. He closed the first half with a flourish, passing to Clark, whose 3-pointer as time expired pushed the Cavaliers' lead to 44-22.

"Guys did a great job of making shots around me," Jerome said.

Many of those shots came from beyond the arc. Virginia was 10 for 14 from long range in the first half and 13 of 24 for the game. Jerome had a game-high four treys, and Guy and Clark made three apiece.

The Hokies heated up offensively in the second half, shooting 12 of 24 from the floor, but Virginia never grew complacent.

After a 3-pointer by Tech guard Ahmed Hill made it 48-34, the Cavaliers responded with a 13-5 run that included a dunk by the 6-8 Key and two baskets by the 6-10 Salt.

"I think Virginia is incredibly well-coached," Tech head coach Buzz Williams said. "I don't think that they get off track. I think they're very sound fundamentally. Very rarely do they take a forced shot. They're very comfortable late in the clock. So I think that defensively you're stressed from the beginning."

Hunter proved to be an especially difficult matchup for the Hokies. A 6-7, 225-pound redshirt sophomore from Philadelphia, Hunter showed why he's projected to be a first-round NBA draft pick. Splitting time at small forward and power forward, he made 8 of 12 shots from the floor, scored 21 points, grabbed five rebounds and had two assists.

"I thought his versatility was on full display tonight," Bennett said.

For the Cavaliers, it was another memorable night in an arena where they've won 51 of their past 56 conference games.

"We're playing at a good level," Bennett said. "I like what I've seen, and it's been different guys at different times."

Virginia celebrates from the sidelines against Virginia Tech.

Matt Riley

Virginia entertained 14,623 fans in a sold-out John Paul Jones Arena for 40 minutes and then some with an 81-59 humbling of ninth-ranked Virginia Tech on Jan. 15.

Matt Riley

Cavaliers Fall Just Short at Cameron

By Jeff White

January 19, 2019

DURHAM, N.C. — For about six hours Saturday, after Michigan lost at Wisconsin in the early afternoon, there was only one unbeaten team in Division I men's basketball, and that was Virginia.

Had the Cavaliers been a little sharper Saturday night, they might well have maintained that status – and won for the second straight year in storied Cameron Indoor Stadium. But in a rare matchup between top-ranked teams, Duke capitalized on UVA's uncharacteristic breakdowns and prevailed 72-70 before a frenzied sellout crowd at Cameron and an ESPN audience.

"That's a big-time game," Duke head coach Mike Krzyzewski said. "They don't get much better than that ... Every possession was high-level."

Virginia came in ranked No. 4 in The Associated Press poll and No. 1 in the coaches' poll. The Blue Devils are ranked No. 1 by the AP and No. 2 by the coaches, and the game was as fiercely contested as expected.

In the second half alone, there were 12 lead changes. But Duke (15-2 overall, 4-1 ACC) went ahead to stay with 7:28 left on a drive by freshman RJ Barrett. The Wahoos (16-1, 4-1) battled to the end, but their lapses, especially on defense, proved costly.

The Blue Devils shot 63.2 percent from the floor in the second half. For the game, they had 10 offensive rebounds and 13 second-chance points, to seven and eight for Virginia.

"I told our guys in the locker room, it wasn't our effort," UVA head coach Tony Bennett said. "It was just enough possessions where we were a bit unsound. We didn't get a block out or we reached on the ball or had a careless turnover. To beat a team like Duke in this setting, you've got to be at an A or an A-minus in those areas. We were a little unsound."

For the game, UVA outshot Duke from the floor, 52.8 percent to 51 percent. But Virginia's inability to keep the 6-7, 202-pound Barrett and his 6-7, 285-pound classmate, Zion Williamson, out of the lane led to one free throw after another for the Blue Devils. Duke struggled from the line, making only 18 for 31 attempts, but its 72 points were the most UVA has allowed this season.

Moreover, Duke had 15 fast-break points, the most the Cavaliers have given up this season.

"We're a solid defensive team, but tonight we were not solid enough," Bennett said. "and that hurts. Large credit [goes to Duke's] play and their ability, but we have to be better in that setting, I believe."

Two players – Barrett (30) and Williamson (27) – accounted for nearly 80 percent of the Blue Devils' points. Between them, they shot 25 free throws.

"They're easily one of the best tandems I've ever played against," Virginia junior Kyle Guy said.

"It was kind of tough keeping them out of the paint," Virginia redshirt sophomore De'Andre Hunter. "Our defense wasn't that great today, so they got a lot of open looks."

Four players scored in double figures for Virginia: Hunter (18 points), Guy (14), Jerome (14) and Key (11). Hunter closed the scoring with a jumper as time expired.

Inside the arc, the Cavaliers were almost impossible to stop, making 25 of 36 shots (69.4 percent). From 3-point range, though, the 'Hoos were only 3 of 17.

"I think we need to find ways to win even when our [perimeter] shots aren't going in," Guy said. "I think there's a lot of shots we wish we could take back, but we'll learn from this game."

The loss ended UVA's run of 12 consecutive ACC road wins, the fourth-longest such streak in league history.

"We'll grow from it," Bennett said.

Guy said: "We'll be just fine. We'll bounce back from this."

Right: The Cameron Crazies give Ty Jerome an earful as he inbounds the ball.

Associated Press

Duke freshman Zion Williamson crashes into two Virginia defenders on a drive to the basket.

Matt Riley

'Hoos Stumble in Rematch

By Jeff White

February 9, 2019

CHARLOTTESVILLE — On the game's first possession, one of Duke's four fabulous freshmen, RJ Barrett, hit a 3-pointer from the left wing.

It was a sign of things to come in an ACC men's basketball game that played out in improbable fashion.

Third-ranked UVA entered the contest leading the nation in 3-point field-goal percentage defense (24.7). Second-ranked Duke was ranked 13th among ACC teams in 3-point field goal percentage (30.8).

So what happened Saturday night at John Paul Jones Arena, with ESPN's College GameDay crew on site?

The Blue Devils made 13 of 21 shots from beyond the arc – 61.9 percent – and never trailed in an 81-71 victory before a sellout crowd that included LeBron James and his Los Angeles Lakers teammates Rajon Rondo and Kentavious Caldwell-Pope.

The 81 points are the most UVA (20-2 overall, 8-2 ACC) has given up this season, as are the 13 treys. Virginia, which prides itself on its transition defense, also allowed 17 fast-break points and turned the ball over 14 times. The Wahoos came in averaging nine turnovers per game, the fewest of any team in Division I.

"I told our guys after [the game], for us to beat a team like Duke, the way they're playing, we are going to have to play a cleaner game in a few areas.," Virginia head coach Tony Bennett said.

When these teams met at Cameron Indoor Stadium last month, the Blue Devils prevailed 72-70, but they were only 2 for 14 from 3-point range. They made 8 for 11 shots from beyond the arc in the first half alone Saturday.

"It's the best we've shot from the 3-point line," Duke head coach Mike Krzyzewski said, "and obviously that's a huge difference."

So, too, was his team's ability to score in transition.

"Look, it's a lot better to get points against [the Cavaliers] when their defense isn't set up," Krzyzewski said. "That helped us tremendously."

In Durham last month, the 'Hoos made only 3 of 17 shots from 3-point range. They were significantly better in that area Saturday night – 10 for 24 – but couldn't keep pace with Duke (21-2, 9-1). The Devils weren't as effective inside the arc as they'd been at Cameron, where Barrett scored a game-high 30 points, but that didn't matter, given their 3-point prowess. UVA placed extra emphasis on plugging gaps in its trademark Pack Line defense, and that gave Duke a little more room on the perimeter.

"We did a much better job in the gap, and they didn't get as many driving lanes," Virginia guard Kyle Guy said, "but when you hit 13 threes, you're going to be hard to beat."

Bennett said: "I thought that we were a little slow to our closeouts. We really tried to keep [Duke] out of the lane and jam the lane. We probably over-corrected in terms of that."

Freshmen accounted for all but seven of Duke's points. Barrett, a 6-8 swingman, led all scorers with 26 points, 6-7 forward Zion Williams had 18, 6-8 swingman Cam Reddish had 17, and 6-2 guard Tre Jones had 13. Jones, who missed the first UVA-Duke game with an injury, also had six rebounds, a game-high seven assists and two steals.

"Tre Jones makes them a different team," Bennett said. "He brings a level of toughness and ball-handling, sureness, touch in the paint, and then defensively, he'll get after you. My hat goes off to a team that played very well today."

Junior guards Ty Jerome and Guy led Virginia with 16 points apiece.

The 'Hoos never quit. A De'Andre Hunter trey made it a five-point game with 5:24 left, but they drew no closer the rest of the way.

Krzyzewski said: "Whenever [Virginia] kind of had a run, one of our guys answered ... Not one guy, but they kind of took turns doing it. Like a counterpunch."

Williamson, a freakish athlete who weighs 285 pounds, had a game-high three blocks. Most memorable was the one, on a Hunter 3-point attempt, that Williamson swatted deep into the stands.

"There's two people in the world maybe that can make those plays, and they were both in our gym tonight," Bennett said with a rueful smile, referring to Williamson and James.

As NBA legend LeBron James looked on, the Duke Blue Devils, led by Zion Williamson, beat the Cavaliers for the second time in the regular season.

Matt Riley

Road Warriors Rally for Thrilling Win

By Jeff White

February 11, 2019

CHAPEL HILL, N.C. — Less than 48 hours after losing to second-ranked Duke in a nationally televised game at John Paul Jones Arena, the Virginia Cavaliers took the court against another national power, again on ESPN, but this time on the road, without a sellout crowd cheering them on.

And so fourth-ranked UVA steeled itself for its matchup with eighth-ranked North Carolina at the 21,750-seat Dean E. Smith Center.

Not since the 2016-17 season has Virginia dropped back-to-back games. The fourth-ranked Wahoos were in danger of doing so Monday night, when UNC went on a 17-3 run in the second half, but they never panicked.

Stay calm, junior guard Ty Jerome told his teammates, and they followed his instructions.

"That's just the way we're wired," junior guard Kyle Guy said.

After UNC went up 55-48 with 7:49 to play, Guy hit a 3-pointer, and the comeback was on. Three more treys followed for the Cavaliers, including two by Guy in the final two minutes, as they pulled away for a 69-61 victory, silencing a partisan crowd of 21,386 that included former Carolina great Michael Jordan.

"I really challenged them hard before the game," UVA head coach Tony Bennett said. "During the day, we talked about what this meant and responding the right way to a hard-fought loss, and I think they did."

The 'Hoos (21-2 overall, 9-2 ACC) hit 11 of 20 attempts from 3-point range and shot 53.3 percent overall. At the other end, their Pack Line defense held UNC (19-5, 9-2) to 35.4-percent accuracy from the floor.

The Tar Heels turned their 16 offensive rebounds into 15 second-chance points. But the Cavaliers, on a night when they made only 10 of 18 free throws, tightened up when they needed to, on both offense and defense. They finished with 10 turnovers, but none came in the final 12 minutes.

"We had some chances to win the game," UNC head coach Roy Williams said, "but they made the plays down the stretch and we didn't. I think their defense was better than our offense. Their offense was better than our defense. We had a great run for eight to 10 minutes and things were going our way. After that it got a lot more difficult, and you've got to give them credit for making it a lot more difficult."

Heroes abounded for UVA in this one. The 6-2 Guy hit 5 of 9 shots from beyond the arc and finished with 20 points. Redshirt sophomore forward De'Andre Hunter matched Guy's scoring output – he was 7 for 10 from the floor, including 3 for 3 from long range – and played exceptional defense on UNC standouts Luke Maye and Coby White.

Maye, who on Monday afternoon was named ACC player of the week, missed 8 of 10 shots from the floor against UVA and finished with four points, 11 under his average. White led the Tar Heels with 17 points but missed 13 of 19 shots from the floor.

UVA forward Mamadi Diakite, who missed most of the Duke game after knocking heads with Hunter, a collision that opened a sizable cut inside the 6-9 redshirt junior's mouth, contributed six points and four blocked shots. Junior forward Braxton Key grabbed a team-high six rebounds, and freshman guard Kihei Clark's on-ball pressure helped the Cavaliers build a 36-29 half-time lead.

And then there was the 6-5 Jerome. Still slowed by the back injury he suffered Jan. 29 at NC State, he totaled 15 points, 11 assists, four rebounds and only two turnovers.

"That says a lot," Bennett said. "He was really good once he got settled in, and he's not 100 percent -- you can see that -- but he's tough. He's a warrior, and I love what he did."

The Tar Heels, who came in averaging 88.3 points per game, scored only two in the final 4:40 Monday night.

"We knew we had to get stops to win the game," Hunter said. "They went on a little run and the crowd was going crazy, but we have experienced guys, and we just knew what we had to do to pull out the win."

Right: De'Andre Hunter scored 20 points against the Tar Heels.

Matt Riley

Jay Huff celebrates a basket against North Carolina on Feb. 11.

Matt Riley

'Hoos Complete Sweep of Hokies

By Jeff White

February 18, 2019

BLACKSBURG — At the half, third-ranked Virginia led 20th-ranked Virginia Tech by three points Monday night, not the worst situation in which a visiting basketball team can find itself at Cassell Coliseum.

Based on UVA head coach Tony Bennett's halftime remarks, however, it "was kind of hard to remember we were up," junior guard Ty Jerome said, smiling. "He really gave it to us."

Bennett had reason to be upset. Lapses marred the Cavaliers' first 20 minutes, and if not for the sharp-shooting of junior guard Kyle Guy, who scored 17 first-half points, they might have faced a substantial deficit.

"We weren't sharp defensively," Bennett said. "We were loose with the ball. We were too finesse. And then in the second half it turned in the right direction."

The result was a 64-58 victory for UVA, which swept its regular-season series with Tech and clinched a point in the schools' Commonwealth Clash competition. Bennett improved his record against the Hokies to 14-6.

"I liked our second half," he said. "It wasn't perfect, but I liked how [Virginia's players] responded. I did not like our first half at all."

Guy made 6 of 13 shots from beyond the arc and finished with 23 points to lead the Wahoos, who for the second straight week won on the road against a ranked opponent on ESPN's Big Monday showcase.

"We'll take the win no matter how it comes," Guy said after his third consecutive game with at least 20 points. "We're

a gritty team and a tough team. We had a couple mental lapses, but nothing we can't fix."

Also scoring in double figures for UVA (23-2 overall, 11-2 ACC) were Jerome (16 points) and redshirt sophomore forward De'Andre Hunter (10). Redshirt junior post player Mamadi Diakite contributed eight points, six rebounds and two blocked shots, and junior forward Braxton Key hit two clutch treys in the final six minutes.

"They showed some toughness in the second half," Bennett said of his players.

For the sixth straight game, Tech (20-6, 9-5) was without its All-ACC point guard, senior Justin Robinson, who was on crutches Monday night, with his left foot in a protective boot.

Even with Robinson sidelined, the Hokies have continued to lead the ACC in field-goal percentage and 3-point field-goal percentage. But they struggled against the Cavaliers' Pack Line defense, making only 3 of 28 shots (10.7 percent) from 3-point range and 23 of 58 (39.7 percent) overall.

"All credit to them defensively," Virginia Tech head coach Buzz Williams said.

The 'Hoos, who hammered the Hokies 81-59 at John Paul Jones Arena last month, were far from flawless in the rematch. They turned the ball over 13 times and gave up 21 second-chance points. But Jerome and Guy typically thrive in pressure situations, and they delivered again Monday night.

After the Hokies scored five straight points to cut the Cavaliers' lead in half, Jerome pulled up for a 3-pointer from the

deep left wing, directly in front of the visitors' bench. It dropped through to push Virginia' lead back to eight and silence the Tech fans in the crowd of 9,275.

"It definitely was contested," Jerome said, "but the shot clock's winding down, and my teammates believe in me, and Coach believes in me. He gives me the freedom to be aggressive at the right times, and I just took advantage of it, and the shot went in."

Bennett said: "He's made a lot of those. He's so competitive, and he's won us a lot of games."

The Cavaliers extended their lead to 13 with 5:50 to play on the first of Key's treys, but the Hokies responded with four straight points. Again, Jerome stopped their run, this time on a drive from the right wing.

Tech rallied yet again, cutting its deficit to seven with 2:34 remaining, only to see Guy take a pass from Jerome and knock down his sixth 3-pointer. A three-point play by Tech guard Ahmed Hill made it 61-54 with 1:25 left, but Diakite passed to Key for a trey that effectively sealed the victory for Virginia.

Key had made only one 3-pointer in UVA's previous eight games.

Against Virginia Tech, Key "moved well, he made a couple nice passes, and then we needed those 3s to go in," Bennett said, "because they were really keying on Ty and on Kyle."

Right: Kyle Guy has a message for the Tech fans after dropping a three.

Matt Riley

The Cavaliers were all smiles after downing the Hokies on the road.

Matt Riley

Cavaliers Send Salt Out on High Note at JPJ

By Jeff White

March 9, 2019

CHARLOTTESVILLE — Had Tony Bennett chosen to climb the ladder last to cut down the final strand of net Saturday evening, nobody in John Paul Jones Arena would have given it a second thought. Bennett, after all, is the architect of one of the nation's premier basketball programs.

But Virginia's head coach wanted his team's only senior, a beloved figure inside and outside JPJ, to have that honor. And so after Bennett descended the ladder, he handed the scissors to Jack Salt, who added the exclamation point to the celebration that followed second-ranked UVA's 73-68 win over Louisville.

To the delight of the thousands of fans who stayed in their seats after the final horn sounded, Salt held the net aloft in triumph, as his teammates and coaches beamed on the court around him.

Salt, who redshirted as a freshman in 2014-15, said he was thinking that it "was amazing just to be a part of this team. I've been here for five years. I've been here awhile. The bond I have shared with the players and the coaches is something I'll never forget."

With the victory, the Cavaliers (28-2, 16-2) clinched their fourth ACC regular-season title in six years. But their focus coming into the regular-season finale, junior guard Ty Jerome said, was on sending Salt, a 6-10 center from New Zealand, out on a high note in his final game at JPJ.

"That's what we talked about before the game," Jerome said. "We didn't talk about the title. We talked about sending him off the right way, because of all that he's done for this program, all he's done for each of us, and just who he is as a person."

Salt said: "That means a lot. I've built such a good relationship with all the guys here, and that's probably the biggest thing I'm going to take away from my five years, just the friends and the family I've made."

Junior guard Kyle Guy echoed Jerome's comments when asked about Salt, who's started 103 games in his UVA career.

"He's such a servant, so humble and doesn't ask for any recognition," Guy said. "His legacy is far beyond the basketball court. He's meant so much to us as a role model and a leader and a teammate and brother."

Second-half comebacks have been a trademark of this UVA team. In the past month, the 'Hoos have rallied to win at North Carolina, at Louisville, and at Syracuse.

Virginia found itself down again Saturday against Louisville (19-12, 10-8), which opened the second half with a 14-4 run to take a 47-40 lead. As usual, the Cavaliers refused to panic.

Guy hit a 3-pointer, Jerome scored on a layup, and 6-9 redshirt junior Mamadi Diakite dunked (off one of Jerome's game-high six assists) to make it 47-47. The Cardinals fought back and opened a six-point lead with 10:43 to play, only to see UVA rally again.

Virginia went ahead for good on two free throws by Jerome with 5:34 remaining. That started an 11-2 run for the Cavaliers.

"The last three, four minutes, they looked like a team that had been there before," Louisville head coach Chris Mack said. "We're getting there."

The victory was UVA's ninth straight over Louisville. When the teams met Feb. 23 at the KFC Yum! Center, Virginia won 64-52 despite making only 2 of 17 shots from 3-point range. Neither Guy nor Jerome, who was recovering from a back injury, had a trey in that game.

"After I shot so badly at their place, I was really excited to play them again," Jerome said Saturday.

He dominated the rematch. The 6-5 Jerome finished with 24 points, six assists, four rebounds and a game-high two steals. He had only one turnover.

"Ty Jerome was so complete," said Bennett, for whom there are few higher compliments about a basketball player.

Jerome hit three treys Saturday, as did Guy, who finished with 13 points. Redshirt sophomore De'Andre Hunter, who came in averaging 15.4 points per game, missed 10 of 13 shots from the floor, but 6-8 junior Braxton Key and 7-1 redshirt sophomore Jay Huff each contributed nine points off the bench.

Key hit a clutch 3-pointer late in the game, and he also had five rebounds and two blocked shots. Huff made a career-high three 3-pointers – he was perfect from beyond the arc – and his final trey, with 5:08 to play, pushed UVA's lead to 66-62 and elicited an arena-shaking roar from the sellout crowd.

"I think that is the key: having different guys [step up] at different times," Bennett said. "That has to happen for us to be successful in single-elimination tournaments now."

Right: Jack Salt cuts down the last of the net after clinching a share of the ACC title.

Matt Riley

In the final game of the season at John Paul Jones Arena, Virginia won a share of the regular-season ACC Championship, gave senior Jack Salt a deserving sendoff, and left fans wondering if there were more nets left to cut down this season.

Matt Riley

Virginia celebrates as a team with the ACC Championship trophy.

Matt Riley

Hunter Takes Center Stage

By Jeff White

CHARLOTTESVILLE — He's not oblivious to the buzz about his potential as a basketball player. He knows NBA scouts have been – and will continue to be -- fixtures at his games this season. Still, De'Andre Hunter says, he's able to block out the external noise when he takes the court for Virginia.

"At the end of the day, you just have to play," Hunter said. "I just try to play and not think about the outside stuff while I'm on the court. I just think of the game, and that's it."

A 6-7, 225-pound forward from Philadelphia, Hunter averaged 9.2 points and 3.3 rebounds as a redshirt freshman last season. He did not start any games – Hunter was the ACC's Sixth Man of the Year -- but as the season progressed many NBA mock drafts began projecting him as a first-round pick.

After considering his options, Hunter decided he wasn't ready for the NBA, and on April 20 he announced on Twitter that he would return to UVA for the 2018-19 academic year.

His stock continues to rise. Hunter finished the national championship season second on the Wahoo team in scoring (15.2 ppg) and rebounds (5.1 per game) while also contributing 22 steals and 22 blocked shots. With a 7-2 wingspan, he's capable of guarding multiple positions, and that adds to his value in head coach Tony Bennett's trademark Pack Line defense.

"Every year you learn more about the defense," Hunter said. "I'm just spreading out. I don't want my man to score, and that's basically my mindset going into every game."

At the Battle 4 Atlantis in Nassau, Bahamas, Hunter was named the tournament's MVP after averaging 19.3 points, 7.7 rebounds and 3.3 assists in UVA's victories over Middle Tennessee, Dayton and Wisconsin.

"That was really encouraging to see," Bennett said, "and I think he enjoys himself out there, and that's even better yet."

Hunter's performance in Nassau earned him another honor: ACC Player of the Week. He shot 61.8 percent from the floor and 81.3 percent from the line in the tournament. In the championship game, Hunter had 20 points and nine rebounds in a 53-46 win over then-No. 25 Wisconsin.

"He's taken his foot off the brake, as we like to say, and we need that," Bennett said.

As he did last season, Hunter split time between small forward and power forward. He shot 52 percent from the floor and 43.8 percent from 3-point range.

"I think he's improved in almost every area," Bennett said. "He understands who he is. He's playing with an assertiveness. He's worked hard on his shot, his body ... I think his ballhandling and his catching and passing, all that's going in the right direction. He seems to have taken a step [with] a year under his belt of experience."

Hunter's 2017-18 season, as UVA fans know all too well, ended before the NCAA tournament. In the ACC tournament semifinals, Hunter broke his left wrist after being hit on a dunk attempt in a 64-58 win over Clemson in Brooklyn, N.Y.

He played through the injury the next night, totaling 10 points and four rebounds in top-seeded UVA's 71-63 win over North Carolina in the ACC title game at Barclays Center. But after the team returned to Charlottesville, Virginia's medical staff determined that Hunter's injury was too serious for him to continue playing.

Without Hunter, top-seeded Virginia had a short stay in the NCAA tournament, losing to No. 16 seed UMBC in the first round. He missed the team's spring workouts while recovering from surgery but returned for the Cavaliers' summer practices.

In August, Hunter was one of 25 college standouts invited to participate in the Nike Basketball Academy in Los Angeles.

Others included Oregon's Bol Bol, Syracuse's Oshae Brissett, Iowa's Tyler Cook, Gonzaga's Rui Hachimura and Virginia Tech's Nickeil Alexander-Walker.

"It was really cool getting to see guys that you probably wouldn't get to play against [during the season] and seeing how good they actually are and playing against them and playing with them," Hunter said. "It was good competition, and being in L.A., of course, was cool, with nice warm weather. It was a great experience."

Right: De'Andre Hunter drives to the basket against Florida State.

Matt Riley

Salt Makes Lasting Impact, On and Off the Court

By Jeff White

CHARLOTTESVILLE — After one of his first days at John Paul Jones Arena, Jack Salt wondered if he'd made a mistake by leaving New Zealand to enroll at the University of Virginia. It was May 2014, and one of his new teammates, Anthony Gill, had just humbled Salt in a workout.

"I thought I was never going to play," Salt recalled.

He pressed on. After redshirting in 2014-15, the 6-10, 250-pound Salt averaged 6.3 minutes per game in 2015-16. He started 34 games in each of the next two seasons and then, in 2018-19, started 29 more for a team that won the program's first NCAA title.

"I've been extremely fortunate just to be on this ride," Salt said. "I never would have thought coming from New Zealand I would finish as a national champion and be a part of so many good teams."

The Cavaliers won 148 games during his five years in the program, a run during which Salt became known for his jarring screens and imposing defensive presence.

"You need players like Jack Salt – and I can go down the list of the players who have been part of this program – to make a national championship team," head coach Tony Bennett said.

In Salt's final season at UVA, his role fluctuated. In only one of the Wahoos' six games in the NCAA tournament did he play more than nine minutes, but he'll never forget that night in Louisville, Ky. In the Elite Eight, he played 34 minutes against Purdue in an overtime win that sent Virginia to the Final Four for the first time since 1984.

"That was awesome for me," Salt said.

Also memorable was his final game at JPJ. With a victory over Louisville, UVA clinched a share of the ACC regular-season title and the No. 1 seed in the conference tournament.

The Cavaliers celebrated by cutting down the net. The honor of snipping the final strand went to Salt, for whom his teammates and coaches speak have enormous respect.

"He's such a servant, so humble and doesn't ask for any recognition," junior guard Kyle Guy said. "His legacy is far beyond the basketball court. He's meant so much to us as a role model and a leader and a teammate and brother."

Salt, who earned a bachelor's in anthropology in 2018, also will leave UVA with a master's from the Curry School of Education. He's distinguished himself in the Charlottesville community, too, regularly stopping by area schools to meet with young students.

"It's so easy to do, and it doesn't take much out of your day, and it really makes somebody else's day, so I try to do that as often as I can," Salt said.

"I'm not a celebrity, but they think I am. It's pretty good just to see smiles on people's faces."

In Auckland, New Zealand, Salt attended Westlake Boys High, a school whose alumni include Kirk Penney, a guard who went on to play two seasons in the NBA. Penney starred for the University of Wisconsin when Bennett was an assistant there, and they're still close.

On Penney's recommendation, Bennett began recruiting the raw but eager-to-learn center. After visiting Charlottesville with his mother, Salt committed to Virginia in September 2013.

Nearly six years later, he celebrated the Cavaliers' NCAA title with his teammates and coaches at Scott Stadium. At an event that drew 21,000 fans, Salt reflected on his college experience.

"I was happy about the decision I made to come to Virginia, happy because of my career," he said. "It's had its ups and downs, but at the end of the day I've been a part of great teams and I've met great people."

Off the court, Jack Salt interacts with children at a Charlottesville elementary school. On the court, he stretched the nets against George Washington early in the season before helping bring them down when the 'Hoos racked up trophy after trophy.

Matt Riley

Humbled, but Healthy

By Jeff White

March 14-15, 2019

CHARLOTTE, N.C. — A year after winning three games in Brooklyn, NY., to capture the ACC tournament, Virginia had a less satisfying experience at the Spectrum Center.

The No. 1 seed for the second straight season, UVA defeated eighth-seeded NC State 76-56 in the first ACC quarterfinal Thursday. In Friday's semifinals, however, the Cavaliers fell 69-59 to fourth-seeded Florida State.

Virginia was looking to advance to the ACC championship game for the fourth time in six seasons. Instead, the Wahoos (29-3) headed back to Charlottesville humbled but, more important, healthy.

They hadn't forgotten the bad fortune that befell them in the 2018 ACC tournament. At Barclays Center, standout forward De'Andre Hunter suffered what turned out to be a season-ending wrist injury. Without him, UVA fell in the first round of the NCAA tournament.

"It's going to be painful not to play [Saturday night]," junior guard Ty Jerome said after the loss to FSU, "but I remember we cut down the nets in the ACC tournament last year and we didn't like the way our season ended.

"So this isn't the end all, be all, by any means."

Redshirt sophomore Jay Huff agreed. "We've been around the block a few times," he said. "I think we'll be just fine. We're going to come out more focused and more determined at our next practice, whenever that is, and be ready to go wherever we play [in the NCAAs]."

The story of UVA's quarterfinal win was the play of 6-10, 250-pound center Jack Salt. A fifth-year senior from New Zealand, Salt entered the postseason never having scored more than 12 points as a Cavalier. He finished with 18 against the Wolfpack, hitting 7 of 8 shots from the floor and 4 of 5 from the free-throw line.

Salt also grabbed six rebounds and blocked a shot in his 26-plus minutes. He contributed three three-point plays to help Virginia defeat the Wolfpack for the eighth straight time.

"It was amazing," said Hunter, who added 16 points. "That's probably the best I've ever seen him play."

During a second half in which Virginia outscored NC State 49-27, Salt had 15 points.

"I've probably been holding him back from scoring, and he's showing it now as we're getting into the postseason," UVA head coach Tony Bennett said, smiling.

Other standouts for the Cavaliers included junior guard Kyle Guy, who made 7 of 9 shots from beyond the arc. Guy, wearing mismatched shoes for the first time in his college career, led all scorers with 29 points.

"The shots that he made were back-breakers," NC State head coach Kevin Keatts said. "I thought Kyle Guy's performance was as good as I've seen this year as far as a guy playing well against us."

Junior guard Ty Jerome was only 1 for 11 from the floor against the Wolfpack, but he had 10 assists and four steals – both game highs -- and grabbed five rebounds.

The next night against Florida State, Jerome was 4 for 13 from the floor and didn't score until the 11:58 mark of the second half. A bigger issue for the Cavaliers, however, was their defense.

In avenging their regular-season loss to Virginia, which won 65-52 at John Paul Jones Arena, the Seminoles shot 56.5 percent from the floor. They outrebounded UVA 35-20.

"They were just the tougher team tonight," Jerome said.

Right: Jack Salt controls the ball against Florida State in the ACC Tournament.

Matt Riley

The 'Hoos huddle up during a loss to
Florida State in the ACC Tournament.

Matt Riley

Dynamic Duo Always Ready to Roll

By Jeff White

CHARLOTTESVILLE — Ty Jerome went first. In September 2014, early in his junior year at Iona Prep in New Rochelle, N.Y., Jerome committed to the University of Virginia, after which a sharp-shooting phenom from Indianapolis started following him on social media.

"I was like, 'Who is this kid?' " Jerome recalled Thursday afternoon.

About six weeks later, that kid, Lawrence Central High junior Kyle Guy, followed Jerome's lead and committed to UVA. Their relationship grew over social media, and they were selected for the same team at the Mary Kline Classic, an all-star game in New Jersey.

"We played together for the first time there," Jerome said.

Guy invited himself to stay at Jerome's house in New York that weekend in May 2015, he recounted with a smile. "We've been friends ever since," said Guy, who like Jerome attended the NBPA Top 100 camp at John Paul Jones Arena in June 2015.

Nearly four years later, it's hard to imagine one on the court without the other. The 6-5 Jerome and the 6-2 Guy started only three games together as freshmen in 2016-17, but since then they've formed one of the nation's premier tandems.

"This is a backcourt of gamers," ESPN analyst Jay Bilas said on Feb. 11 after Virginia rallied to defeat North Carolina in Chapel Hill. "They might not look like they're tough competitors – they look like boy scouts – but, man, they play like they're in a motorcycle gang."

"They're complete," UVA head coach Tony Bennett said about his backcourt. "They obviously can shoot the ball from deep ... but they're capable [also] of putting it on the floor, driving, drawing fouls, or hitting pull-ups, floaters, and they'll make the right passes."

Guy, a third-team All-American for the second year in a row in 2018-19, was also a repeat selection on the All-ACC first team this season. Jerome, who made the All-ACC third team last season, moved up to the second team this year.

"I use them as examples for my young guards to watch those two guys, because they're such big-time winners," Notre Dame head coach Mike Brey said.

"They know who they are, and they play within themselves ... They're assassins and winners. They've had great careers."

Guy, whose release is as quick as that of any college player, averaged a team-high 15.4 points while shooting 42.6 percent from beyond the arc.

His career 3-point shooting percentage (42.5) ranks first all-time both at UVA and in the ACC. He buried a career-high eight treys – one shy of the program record – in Virginia's win over Syracuse at the Carrier Dome in early March.

"Some of the shots Kyle hit were unreal," Jerome said.

Duke's Hall of Fame coach, Mike Krzyzewski, has compared Guy to former ACC great J.J. Redick. Florida State head coach Leonard Hamilton is another fan of No. 5.

Right: Guards Ty Jerome (11) and Kyle Guy during a game against Maryland.

Matt Riley

∞

'This is a backcourt of gamers. They might not look like they're tough competitors — they look like Boy Scouts — but, man, they play like they're in a motorcycle gang.'

ESPN analyst Jay Bilas

"You watch him play on film, and you just don't believe a guy is capable of being that confident when he shoots the ball," Hamilton said.

Jerome led the ACC in assists (6.1 per game). He's first on the team in steals as well and averaged 13.6 points per game. He shot 39.9 percent from 3-point range and has almost unlimited range. He had 202 assists which ranks tied for third all-time for a single season at UVA.

"He's just such a multi-dimensional player," Gardner-Webb head coach Tim Craft said prior to the NCAA tourney opener.

Jerome, who wears jersey No. 11, is a nightmare to defend, Craft said, "because his change of pace is so good and he's such a good shooter. He can shoot it from about 22, 23 feet at a high level. He creates some problems for you defensively just from a one-on-one standpoint, but then in their actions with the pick-and-rolls and the down screens."

Bennett's assistants include Brad Soderberg, who's been head coach at five schools: Loras College, South Dakota State,

Wisconsin, Saint Louis and Lindenwood University. Soderberg played at Wisconsin-Stevens Point for Bennett's father, Dick, and has seen countless talented guards in his three decades in coaching.

Guy and Jerome, Soderberg said, rank among the best.

"I think the first thing that sticks out is their ability to shoot the ball collectively," Soderberg said. "I've seen a lot of combinations of good guards, but seldom do you have to respect both the 1 and the 2 from distance like you have to do with those two guys.

"I think the other thing is that they've logged so many games already.

"Usually guys have to wait their turn, and [Guy and Jerome] didn't have to wait very long. And I think because of the fact that they've played in arguably the best conference in America and played the number of games that they have as a combination, they know what each other's going to do five seconds before they do it."

UVA staff would not have recruited Guy and Jerome had the coaching staff not believed they could become productive players in the ACC.

But did the coaches expect them to be so good so quickly? Maybe not.

"In their sophomore and junior years, they've won 60 basketball games," Soderberg said. "So anyone that says, 'That's exactly what I envisioned,' they're lying to you. But to their credit, they've been very receptive to what Coach Bennett has to offer. He's demanding on guards, because he was an excellent guard himself. He's pressed them, he's worked them hard, and they've accepted it. They've listened to what he's had to say, and I think because of that they've experienced the success that they've had."

Soderberg added one more thing: "What a privilege it's been to be around those two guys."

Right: Kyle Guy (5) and Ty Jerome on the court during the ACC Tournament.

Matt Riley

'Hoos Embrace NCAA Tournament Challenge

By Jeff White

March 17, 2019

CHARLOTTESVILLE —About 30 minutes before the NCAA tournament field was revealed Sunday evening, Virginia junior Kyle Guy stood outside the home locker at John Paul Jones Arena and acknowledged the inevitable.

No matter what seed the Cavaliers received or in which regional they were placed, Guy knew, they would face questions about what happened to them last year.

Want to bring up UVA's historic loss to UMBC in last year's NCAA tournament? Fire away, the All-ACC guard said.

"That's basically what I'm trying to do, just hit it head on," Guy said. "I don't really care what anybody thinks. They can ask what they want. They can say what they want. I still got love for them, and I'm still going to play my game."

Ten minutes into CBS' selection show Sunday night, the Wahoos learned they'd been awarded one of the tournament's four No. 1 seeds for the fourth time in the past six seasons. UVA (29-3), the top seed in the South Region, will meet No. 16 seed Gardner-Webb (23-11) at Colonial Life Arena in Columbia, S.C.

Virginia is in its 10th season under head coach Tony Bennett. This is the Cavaliers' sixth straight trip to the NCAA tournament, a program record.

To be a No. 1 seed "doesn't guarantee you anything, as we know," Bennett said on a teleconference, "but it certainly means it was a heck of a season, and now you get ready to go play against teams that are all playing well."

Last year in Charlotte, N.C., as the basketball world knows, Virginia became the first No. 1 seed to lose to a No. 16 seed in the NCAA tournament, falling to UMBC in the first round.

From that moment, associate head coach Jason Williford said, the 'Hoos became part of history. "So every year at this time it's going to be a circus, it's going to be crazy. We're going to have to answer those questions. You gotta go through it. It's nothing we've run from."

Bennett agreed. "I think that kind of comes with the territory [because of] what happened last year. We certainly have talked about it, and that's been the case all year, whether it's fans or media bringing it up. You answer questions when you get asked, but there's not a whole lot [more] to say about it. I think it's been dealt with. It really is time to play."

The 'Hoos entered last year's NCAAs as ACC tournament champions. Their run in the conference tourney didn't last as long this year. Top-seeded Virginia fell 69-59 to fourth-seeded Florida State in the ACC semifinals in Charlotte.

That ended the Cavaliers' nine-game winning streak. Before returning to Charlottesville, they watched film of the loss to FSU, which shot 56.5 percent from the floor and outrebounded Virginia 35-20.

"It was very evident that we got out-toughed, out-rebounded, out-hustled," Guy said. "All the little things that we take pride in, I think they just did a better job of. And they wanted it more."

The Seminoles "were good, and we got away from our identity defensively," Williford said. "And so we gotta be better at helping each other, we gotta be better on the ball. Some of our ball-screen defense was just not good, the rotations and the weakside stuff.

"There's no need to overreact, but we gotta be ready to defend harder, defend better. I think offensively this group has different weapons and people we can go to, but defensively we gotta kind of get back to some old-school Virginia defensive principles."

Gardner-Webb, which is located in Boiling Springs, N.C., earned an automatic bid to the NCAA tournament by winning the Big South tournament last weekend.

The Runnin' Bulldogs have won 11 of their past 13 games. They lost in early November to VCU and Virginia Tech, teams UVA defeated during the regular season, but they won at Georgia Tech and at Wake Forest in December.

"Looking at their offensive numbers and defensive numbers, I know obviously Gardner-Webb is very good," Bennett said. "There's certainly great respect for them."

For the Cavaliers, who shared the ACC regular-season title with North Carolina, this will be their second game in Columbia in about three months. Virginia defeated South Carolina 69-52 at Colonial Life Arena on Dec. 19.

Seven teams from the ACC earned invitations to the NCAA tournament. Three were awarded No. 1 seeds: Virginia (South), ACC tournament champion Duke (East) and North Carolina (Midwest).

"To get a share of the regular-season conference championship, in a league that has three number ones, that obviously tells you the quality of the league," Bennett said. "I think the ACC obviously is represented well in this tournament and hopefully it does very well, too."

Matt Riley

'Hoos Follow Hunter's Lead in Gritty Win

By Jeff White

March 22, 2019

COLUMBIA, S.C. — Two years and nine months after joining the University of Virginia men's basketball program, De'Andre Hunter finally made his NCAA tournament debut. The Philadelphia native's performance reminded the hoops world how much his absence hurt the Cavaliers in last year's NCAA tourney.

A 6-7, 225-pound swingman who redshirted in 2016-17, Hunter was the ACC's Sixth Man of the Year in 2017-18, only to suffer a season-ending wrist injury in the ACC tournament.

Without him, UVA became the first No. 1 seed in NCAA tourney history to lose to a No. 16 seed, falling to UMBC in the first round last year in Charlotte, N.C.

With him, Virginia, the No. 1 seed in the South Region, overcame a slow start and rallied for a 71-56 victory over 16th-seeded Gardner-Webb at Colonial Life Arena.

Virginia (30-3) advances to meet ninth-seeded Oklahoma (20-13) in the second round.

Like UMBC had been in 2018, Gardner-Webb was significantly smaller than Virginia.

"When you go against these quick teams, you have to sometimes match the quickness to the best of your abilities," said UVA head coach Tony Bennett. "Last year, we didn't have Kihei Clark or De'Andre [against UMBC], so [their presence] allowed us to be a little more versatile to match their quickness and then to switch some of those ball screens."

The Cavaliers weren't that efficient offensively against Gardner-Webb – they committed 15 turnovers and made only 7

of 23 shots from 3-point range – but they dominated around the basket. UVA outrebounded the Runnin' Bulldogs 35-21 and made 21 of 31 shots inside the arc.

Hunter, a first-team All-ACC selection who's also the conference's defensive player of the year, led the way. He finished with 23 points, three rebounds, two blocked shots and one assist.

"He's a monster for us to guard," Gardner-Webb head coach Tim Craft said, "and [for] most of the country."

"He's ridiculous," said 7-1 redshirt sophomore Jay Huff, who enrolled at UVA in June 2016 with Hunter and guards Kyle Guy and Ty Jerome.

"He was tremendous today," Guy said.

Heading into his NCAA tourney debut, Hunter said afterward, "I was really excited, probably the most excited I've been in a while for a game."

No. 12 rarely shows much emotion on the floor, but this was not just another game. He celebrated after a momentum-changing dunk that cut Gardner-Webb's lead to 38-36 with 17:28 remaining. About 70 seconds later, Hunter gave the 'Hoos their first lead, at 39-38, with a three-point play. They never trailed again.

"In the second half it was win or lose," Hunter said. "If we lose, we're not playing again, so we just knew we had to come out and fight, and that's what we did."

Redshirt junior Mamadi Diakite (17) and Jerome (13) also scored in double figures for UVA, and Guy added eight points.

But don't be fooled by the margin of victory. This win did not come easily for the Cavaliers.

With 6:30 left in the opening half, the Runnin' Bulldogs led 30-16 – that matched UVA's largest deficit of the season -- and their fans' cheers threatened to shake the building. Columbia is about 125 miles from Gardner-Webb's campus in Boiling Springs, N.C., and in "some ways it felt like a road game [for UVA] with the crowd, too," Bennett said.

It was an 11-point game with 2:25 to play in the first half, but freshman point guard Clark passed to Huff for a dunk that made it 36-27. Clark then sank a long 3-pointer to cut Gardner-Webb's lead to 36-30. That was the score at halftime, and UVA regrouped in the locker room.

Getting it "back to a six-point game was pivotal for us," Bennett said, "because Gardner-Webb's good."

The 'Hoos kept coming after intermission. A 12-0 run gave them a 44-38 lead, and they followed that with an 11-0 run capped by junior forward Braxton Key's 3-pointer with 10:13 remaining.

"I thought the guys just kept plugging," Bennett continued, "and Gardner-Webb missed some shots. Maybe they got fatigued. I thought the resolve of our team was good to weather that storm and have a good second half."

Right: Virginia tips off the NCAA Tournament against Gardner-Webb.

Matt Riley

Right: After falling behind early, Virginia fought back for a hard-earned first-round victory over Gardner-Webb.

Far right: The Cavaliers and coach Tony Bennett share a laugh as they walk to the media room following their first round win in the NCAA Tournament.

Matt Riley

Next Stop on Cavaliers' Journey: Sweet Sixteen

By Jeff White

March 24, 2019

COLUMBIA, S.C. — Make no mistake, the University of Virginia men's basketball team is delighted to be headed to the Sweet Sixteen for the first time since 2016. But the Cavaliers are far from satisfied. They made that clear in their postgame comments at Colonial Life Arena.

"The journey's not done yet," redshirt junior Mamadi Diakite said after UVA, the South Region's No. 1 seed, defeated ninth-seeded Oklahoma 63-51 in the NCAA tournament's second round.

"We're going to enjoy this win and enjoy moving on, but the job's not done," junior forward Braxton Key said.

Next up for Virginia (31-3), which has tied the program record for victories in a season set in 2017-18, is a third-round date with 12th-seeded Oregon (25-12) in Louisville, Ky.

For the Wahoos, their latest victory means "another week, [another] opportunity to play with the teammates you love, for the coaches you love, and for the fans you love," junior guard Ty Jerome said. "But we're nowhere near relaxed, nowhere near satisfied. We're not even close to our end goal."

The 'Hoos were noticeably tight in their first-round game against No. 16 seed Gardner-Webb, and understandably so considering what transpired in their last NCAA tourney opener against UMBC.

Against Oklahoma (20-14), the vibe was different.

"There's pressure and excitement and tension to try to advance in this tournament, that's always there, but it was a differ-ent feel against Gardner-Webb," head coach Tony Bennett said. "No [other] college basketball team, really in the history of the game, has had to go through that. I think those guys will have that as something they can always draw upon to say we faced a giant and battled through it."

The Cavaliers scored the game's first seven points, prompting a timeout by Oklahoma head coach Lon Kruger.

"Seeing shots go in at the start was big," redshirt sophomore Jay Huff said. "That never hurts. But I just think after the first game Friday, we were all a little more relaxed, a little relieved."

"We just wanted to make sure we took care of business the entire 40 minutes this time," junior guard Kyle Guy said.

The 'Hoos didn't sustain their initial surge. After putting up seven points in the first 103 seconds, they scored only two over the next seven-plus minutes. But the Sooners didn't fully capitalize. The Cavaliers eventually found their rhythm again and went into halftime with a 31-22 lead.

"We were comfortable out there," redshirt sophomore De'Andre Hunter said.

Two days after scoring 95 points in a first-round win over eighth-seeded Mississippi, Oklahoma encountered infinitely more resistance against Virginia's Pack Line defense. For the game, the Sooners shot only 36.5 percent from the floor.

"We were keeping them out of the lane, and we were getting to the shooters," Hunter said.

Bennett, pleased with the 6-9 Diakite's play against Gard-ner-Webb, started him in Jack Salt's place. It was the first start since Feb. 27 for Diakite, who turned in a sparkling performance, scoring 14 points (on 7-for-9 shooting), tying his career high with nine rebounds, and blocking three shots.

"I was locked in, and I was trying to respond to the challenge Coach gave me," Diakite said. "He started me tonight, and I wanted to prove to him that I was ready to play."

Virginia's attributes include its balance and depth. On a night when All-ACC guard Kyle Guy, one of the nation's premier outside shooters, was 0 for 10 from beyond the 3-point arc, the Cavaliers weren't seriously threatened over the final 25 minutes.

"It just shows how deep we are, how much we want to win, and how much none of us really care about scoring," said Guy, who finished with a season-low four points. "We just want to win."

In addition to Diakite, Jerome (12 points) and Hunter (10 points) scored in double figures for UVA. Key and freshman point guard Kihei Clark added nine points apiece, and Huff chipped in five points in his seven-minute stint in the first half.

"We took whatever the defense gave us," Guy said. "I don't really care if I score or not. I want to go to the Sweet Sixteen."

Clark agreed. "You dream of this your whole life. It's great to advance."

Right: Jay Huff dunks against Oklahoma during a round of 32 victory.

Matt Riley

Right: Oklahoma was supposed to provide the first real test of the NCAA Tournament for Virginia in the round of 32 at Columbia, S.C., but the 'Hoos passed with flying colors.

Far right: Ty Jerome celebrates during the 63-51 win over the Sooners.

Matt Riley

'Hoos Battle Their Way Into Elite Eight

By Jeff White

March 28, 2019

LOUISVILLE, KY. — They waited all day and well into the night Thursday, and then they had to endure a 35-minute delay when the game between Purdue and Tennessee went into overtime at the KFC Yum! Center.

By the time the Virginia Cavaliers made it back to their downtown hotel, it was 1:30 a.m. If they were exhausted, though, they were also elated. After ousting Oregon in the NCAA tournament's Sweet Sixteen, UVA is a win away from the Final Four.

"I can't tell you how thankful and excited I am," head coach Tony Bennett said at his postgame press conference.

One more win over third-seeded Purdue (26-9) would send the Cavaliers to the Final Four for the first time since 1984.

"I'd be lying if I said my mind hasn't wandered there from time to time," UVA junior guard Kyle Guy said, "but at the same time I'm trying to stay in the moment ... I'm just so excited right now."

In a game that matched two of the nation's premier defensive teams, UVA rallied to beat Oregon 53-49. The Cavaliers shot 35.7 percent from the floor; the Ducks, 37.8 percent.

"You hang on and hang your hat on that defense," Bennett said, "and hopefully you get enough offense. Ugly is in the eye of the beholder. Maybe it wasn't great, but I thought it was pretty good looking for us defensively."

Oregon, seeking to become the first No. 12 seed to knock off a No. 1 seed in NCAA tournament history, appeared to be in position to do so after taking a 45-42 lead with 5:39 to play on forward Louis King's second straight 3-pointer.

The Wahoos didn't panic. A trey by the unflappable Kihei Clark, a 5-9 freshman from Los Angeles, made it 45-45, and then the 'Hoos went ahead to stay on a catch-and-shoot 3-pointer by junior guard Ty Jerome with 3:33 remaining.

Such cold-blooded shots are a Jerome trademark, as teammate Mamadi Diakite noted.

"In those situations, you know, most people will not shoot the ball, because they're a little nervous," said Diakite. "But that's not the type of guy he is. He's very cold. He's very confident."

With 27 seconds left, Guy found redshirt sophomore forward De'Andre Hunter alone under the basket for a layup that made it 50-45.

Oregon's only points in the final 5:38 came on free throws in the last 17 seconds. The Ducks (25-13), who entered on a 10-game winning streak, missed their final five shots from the floor and turned the ball over twice late against Virginia's Pack Line defense.

"I think we played great," said Hunter, the ACC's defensive player of the year. "We were communicating, we were scrambling, keeping guys in front, rebounding. We were doing all the things we practice every day. I think those last five minutes just shows how great we can be."

The Ducks start four 6-9 players, and their length gave the Cavaliers' problems. With about six minutes left in the first half, Virginia was 4 for 21 from the floor and trailed 16-10. But the first of Clark's three 3-pointers started a 10-0 run, and UVA went into the break up 30-22.

Guy, who this week was named a third-team All-American, has been mired in an uncharacteristic shooting slump during this NCAA tournament. In Virginia's second-round win over Oklahoma, he was 0 for 10 from 3-point range, and Guy missed his first five shots from beyond the arc against Oregon.

At the 17:24 mark of the second half, however, Guy finally saw a 3-pointer go down. That made it 33-27, and then Clark fed Hunter for a layup to push Virginia's lead to eight. But the game never became one-sided. Oregon answered with seven straight points, and the teams went back and forth for most of the final 12 minutes.

"It was just kind of a slugfest, it felt like it," Bennett said, "and it was sort of last man standing."

Right: UVA forward Mamadi Diakite goes head-to-head with Oregon's Ehab Amin

Matt Riley

Twelfth-seeded Oregon gave Virginia its toughest test so far in the NCAA Tournament, but the Cavaliers used a smothering defense to seal a 53-49 win and advance to the Elite Eight.

Top images and bottom left: Associated Press

Bottom right: Matt Riley

The sidelines erupt during Virginia's
Sweet 16 win over Oregon.

Matt Riley

Minneapolis, Here We Come!

By Jeff White

March 30, 2019

LOUISVILLE, KY. — For the University of Virginia basketball fans who soaked in every second of the postgame celebration at the KFC Yum! Center, the enduring image figures to be the sight of Tony Bennett atop a ladder, exulting as he waved the net that signified a milestone for his program.

But so many moments led to the jubilant scene that followed top-seeded UVA's 80-75 overtime win over third-seeded Purdue in the South Region final.

Where to begin? With Kyle Guy's second-half tour de force? Ty Jerome's all-around brilliance? Kihei Clark's poise under pressure as the final seconds ticked away in regulation? Jack Salt's relentless rebounding? Mamadi Diakite's season-saving shot? The De'Andre Hunter basket that put UVA ahead for good in overtime?

All of those merit mention, but let's go back even further: to March 30, 2009, a day that changed the fortunes of a once-elite program that had sunk into mediocrity.

On that day, Bennett agreed to leave Washington State, where he'd succeeded his father, Dick, as head coach, and come to UVA. Ten years later – to the day – Bennett guided Virginia to its first Final Four appearance since 1984.

"It's a pretty good 10-year anniversary gift, for sure," Bennett said.

In 10 seasons under Bennett, UVA has become an ACC power and a fixture in the NCAA tournament. But his teams had often underachieved on the college game's biggest stage, most memorably in 2018. UVA has now exorcised that demon.

The Wahoos (33-3) are headed to Minneapolis, where they'll meet Auburn in the NCAA semifinals. This will be the third Final Four in program history for Virginia, which advanced twice under head coach Terry Holland (1981 and '84).

"I'm so happy for my teammates and my coaches and for myself to be able to break through in the way that we did this year," Guy said. "Not only did we silence [Bennett's] critics, we silenced our own, and we're so grateful for our fans that traveled and have always believed in us."

Jerome added: "To be the team that gets him to the Final Four, I think that's what means the most. But he's believed in every single one of us. He has our best interest at heart, on and off the court. And he's a great person."

Bennett was a volunteer manager on his father's Wisconsin team that in 2000 defeated Purdue in the Elite Eight to advance to the Final Four. Bennett's parents, his wife, his children, his sisters and other relatives were at the game Saturday to provide emotional and vocal support.

"I'm so thankful," Bennett said after praising his staff. "I don't deserve the credit. I don't care about the critics. I don't even pay attention to that. I really don't. I just know it was really hard to lose in the first round [to UMBC]. It stung. It was a painful gift. It was so humbling, but it drew me and drew our team closer in a way we couldn't have [done otherwise]."

"It's amazing," Hunter said. "We knew what we were capable of at the start of this year. We put the past behind us, we put that game behind us, and we just focused on this year."

If not for an improbable sequence in the final seconds of regulation, Virginia's season would have ended in the Elite Eight.

After Purdue went up 69-67 on guard Carsen Edwards' 10th 3-pointer of the game – no, that's not a misprint – UVA turned the ball over at the other end.

Edwards then missed a 3-point attempt, but Grady Eifert grabbed the offensive rebound for the Boilermakers (26-10) to extend the possession. Virginia was forced to foul, sending Purdue guard Ryan Cline to the line for a one-and-one with 16.9 seconds to play.

Cline hit his first free throw to make it 70-67, but he missed the second and UVA rebounded. The Boilermakers did not want to give up a game-tying 3-pointer, so with 5.9 seconds remaining they fouled Jerome. He made the front end of his one-and-one, but his second shot hit the front of the rim and bounced off.

Right: Mamadi Diakite beats the buzzer to tie the game and force overtime against Purdue.

Associated Press

'It was unbelievable.
I don't know how to talk about it.'

Mamadi Diakite, on his game-tying shot against Purdue
that sent the game to overtime.

"I didn't really miss it on purpose," Jerome said later. "I short-armed it."

Had the Boilermakers collected the rebound, they almost certainly would have also secured their first trip to the Final Four since 1980. But the 6-9 Diakite batted the ball into the backcourt – one of 17 offensive rebounds for UVA in this game – and Clark tracked it down near the near 3-point line.

Three seconds remained. On the Virginia bench, Hunter feared the worst. "I was like, 'The game's over,'" he told reporters later.

Ah, but it wasn't, thanks to Clark, a fearless freshman who made what Jerome called "the play of the century."

Clark caught up to the ball, turned around, took two quick dribbles and fired a one-handed pass to Diakite, whose 12-foot jumper barely beat the buzzer to send the game into overtime.

"It was unbelievable," Diakite said. "I don't know how to talk about it."

In overtime, Virginia trailed 72-70 and then 73-72. Two free throws by Hunter at the 1:42 mark put the Cavaliers up 74-73, but Edwards answered with his 41st and 42nd points with 42 seconds left.

This Elite Eight game did not produce a vintage outing from Hunter, but the second-team All-American delivered in OT. His layup with 26.8 seconds remaining gave Virginia a 76-75 lead.

Edwards missed another 3-point attempt, and the 6-2 Guy came down with the last of his career-high 10 rebounds.

Purdue fouled Guy, who calmly sank two free throws to make it 78-75 with 5.7 seconds to play. The Boilermakers turned the ball over on their next possession, and Clark sealed the victory with two free throws with 1.3 seconds left.

"Amazing feeling," said Clark, who finished with five assists, three rebounds, two points, one steals and no turnovers. "I'm at a loss for words right now."

The team's veterans had more to say after what was, for all intents and purposes, a road game for the 'Hoos. The large majority of the fans in the crowd of 21,623 came to cheer for the Boilermakers, but that didn't faze Virginia.

"Calm is contagious," Guy likes to say, and the Cavaliers never panicked Saturday night, even after Purdue hit seven 3-pointers (in 10 attempts) in the first 12 minutes.

At halftime, Guy was 0 for 3 from beyond the arc, which made him 3 for 29 from long range in the NCAA tournament. But Purdue's lead was only one, 30-29, and the Cavaliers were confident Guy would eventually regain his shooting touch.

It happened in a flash. In the second half, the 6-2 Guy, who grew up in Indianapolis and was a Purdue recruiting target, hit his first four shots from beyond the arc. He finished with a team-high 25 points and, with his 10 rebounds, posted his first double-double as a Cavalier.

Four players scored in double figures for UVA: Guy, Jerome (24), Diakite (14) and Hunter (10). Diakite tied his career high with four blocked shots and also had seven rebounds. Jerome had a game-high seven assists to go with five rebounds. Salt, in 34 minutes off the bench, pulled down eight rebounds, five at the offensive end.

For Purdue, the only player to score more than seven points was Edwards, a 6-1 junior whose shot-making ability was mesmerizing. He made 14 of 25 shots from the floor, including 10 of 19 from beyond the arc. His 10 treys are the most ever by a player against UVA.

At times the Cavaliers went big against Edwards, putting the 6-7 Hunter on him, and at times they went small, with the 5-9 Clark. No matter.

"That was the best performance I've ever seen," Jerome said. "That was the best performance I've ever played against. Kihei and Dre are both great on-ball defenders, and he just hit everything. Going to the basket, step-back 3s. Unbelievable. Unbelievable. I told him after the game that he's a hell of a player."

It was, Guy said, a "performance for the ages -- by him and by both teams."

Right: The Cavaliers celebrate Mamadi Diakite's shot that sent the game into overtime.

Matt Riley

Kyle Guy (25 points in the game) locked himself in a second-half duel with Purdue star Carsen Edwards (42 points) before the 'Hoos won in overtime and coach Tony Bennett cut down the nets after winning the South Region in Louisville, Ky.

Matt Riley

Coach Bennett and the Cavaliers celebrate in the locker room after clinching a trip to the Final Four.

Matt Riley

Bennett Sets Standard for 'Hoos

By Jeff White

CHARLOTTESVILLE — The news broke on March 30, 2009, that the University of Virginia had hired Tony Bennett as its men's basketball coach. For UVA fans who didn't follow West Coast hoops closely – which is to say, most of them – the general reaction could be summed up as follows:

Who's Tony Bennett?

It's been years since anybody has asked that question. Bennett has built a national power in Charlottesville, and he's done so while staying true to his values and his faith. The foundation of his program are the biblical pillars of humility, passion, unity, servanthood and thankfulness, and Bennett lives them every day.

"He has such a humble spirit about him," UVA athletic director Carla Williams said.

"Tony is an exceptional leader in every sense of the word, on and off the court," UVA president Jim Ryan said. "He is gracious in defeat and humble in victory."

There may not be a more respected coach in the college game, and that's as much for the manner in which Bennett car-

ries himself as for his considerable acumen as a tactician.

"He's just so humble and genuine," guard Kyle Guy said. "It's never about him. That's why he's such a great leader."

Success did not come immediately for Bennett at UVA, where his record after two years was 31-31.

But over the past six seasons Virginia has won 178 games, captured four ACC regular-season titles and won the conference tournament twice. The Cavaliers have become fixtures in the NCAA tournament, and their long-awaited breakthrough finally came this year.

On March 30, 2019, Bennett guided Virginia to its first Final Four appearance in 35 years. Nine days later, in Minneapolis, Bennett and his players celebrated their crowning achievement: the program's first NCAA championship.

When the final horn sounded at U.S. Bank Stadium, Bennett remained seated for a moment on a stool next to the UVA bench.

"I was overcome with thankfulness and humbled," Bennett said. "It was so improbable how we won these games and all the

things that went on."

The 'Hoos, Bennett said, authored "one of the greatest stories that I've ever seen written, and it'll be told over and over again."

That was not hyperbole. In their first six trips to the NCAA tournament under Bennett, the Cavaliers had advanced past the Sweet Sixteen only once -- in 2016, when they lost in the Elite Eight -- and they'd played poorly in several of their season-ending losses.

The most memorable of those defeats, of course, came in 2018, when Virginia became the first No. 1 seed in NCAA tournament history to lose to a No. 16 seed, falling to UMBC. In the aftermath, critics assailed Bennett, saying his teams didn't have enough offensive punch and that Virginia's Pack Line defense would never be as effective in the NCAA tourney as it was during the regular season.

Right: Tony Bennett follows the action during the national championship game.

Matt Riley

'Tony is an exceptional leader in every sense of the word, on and off the court. He is gracious in defeat and humble in victory.'

Virginia president Jim Ryan

"From a basketball standpoint," Bennett said, "that was such a pivotal moment and devastating in so many ways and humbling, that I knew we had to be there for each other in ways we never would have had that not happened. So it was about sitting together, talking, and just working through stuff and battling through it, and trusting each other."

The Cavaliers drew motivation from several sources, including a TED Talk by a former Methodist minister, Donald Davis, that was titled *How the Story Transforms the Teller*.

The loss to UMBC was "a painful gift," Bennett said. It left a scar, but the Cavaliers refused to let it break them.

"I'm thankful in a way for what happened," Bennett said, "because it drew me closer, most importantly, to my faith in the Lord, drew me closer to my wife and children, just because you realize what's unconditional. In those spots when the world's telling you you're a failure, you're a loser, and you're the worst thing going, and all that stuff, you say, OK, what really matters?"

Bennett grew up around the game. He starred for his father,

Dick, a legendary coach, at Wisconsin-Green Bay, and then played in the NBA for three seasons. Bennett started coaching in New Zealand in the late 1990s but did not plan to stay in the profession.

When he returned to the United States, though, he had a change of heart. In 2000, Bennett was a volunteer manager on his father's Wisconsin team that advanced to the Final Four, and he was hooked.

For the next three seasons, Bennett served as an assistant coach at Wisconsin – for his father, for Brad Soderberg and for Bo Ryan. In 2003, Bennett joined his father's staff at Washington State, where after three seasons he took over as head coach.

In three seasons leading the Cougars, Bennett posted a 69-33 record, with two trips to the NCAA tournament and one to the NIT.

At UVA, his record is 254-89, with seven trips to the NCAA tournament and one to the NIT. And now, after a postseason run that included two miraculous comebacks, Bennett has a national championship.

"He's so far past me that I feel like I'm back in kindergarten," Dick Bennett said.

Soderberg played for Dick Bennett at Wisconsin-Stevens Point and later coached under him at Wisconsin. In 2015, Soderberg left Lindenwood University, where he was head coach, to join Tony Bennett's staff at UVA. He's gained a new appreciation for a friend he's known since Bennett was a boy in Stevens Point.

"I've been around a long time. I've worked with a lot of guys," Soderberg said. "I haven't been with a guy like this. His knowledge of the game, his interaction with players is real and genuine. His disposition on the bench is uncanny. His poise under pressure is unbelievable. You just don't find that."

Virginia found that in March 2009 when then-AD Craig Littlepage and his top assistant, Jon Oliver, persuaded Bennett to leave Washington State. The Cavaliers will be forever grateful.

"We couldn't have done this with any other coach," guard Ty Jerome said.

Top photos: Tony Bennett shares a laugh with Texas Tech coach Chris Beard before answering questions from the media during the Final Four. **Bottom photos:** (l) Bennett and his players joke around prior to the national championship celebration at Scott Stadium; (r) Bennett greets his parents, Dick and Anne, at the team hotel after clinching a trip to the Final Four.

Top left:
Associated Press

All others:
Matt Riley

Embracing the Atmosphere, Avoiding the Distractions

By Jeff White

April 4, 2019

MINNEAPOLIS — Some 70,000 fans will pack U.S. Bank Stadium on Saturday evening for the start of the NCAA men's basketball tournament's Final Four. Once their locker room was opened for interviews Thursday afternoon, Virginia's players might have thought at least that many media members were in town for the event, too, such was the crush of bodies in that confined area.

The Cavaliers didn't seem to mind, though. This was all part of the Final Four experience, they realized, along with the photo and video shoots that had filled their Thursday morning at the Minnesota Vikings' stadium.

"I think the first thing you gotta do is just take a second and enjoy it," junior guard Ty Jerome said. "We worked so hard to be here. Enjoy all the media -- some of it was fun -- and enjoy being here with your brothers and your teammates."

In the first NCAA semifinal Saturday, UVA (33-3) meets Auburn (30-9) at U.S. Bank Stadium. Michigan State (32-6) and Texas Tech (30-6) follow in the second semifinal.

"Watching college basketball [as a boy] and filling out your bracket, you dream of this setting," freshman guard Kihei Clark said.

The Cavaliers arrived in the Twin Cities on Wednesday, as did the other semifinalists, so the players will have plenty of time to get acclimated to their surroundings before the biggest game of their lives tips off Saturday night.

"I think if you show up the day before, then it becomes tough to enjoy the other stuff, because you gotta really lock in immediately," Jerome said. "So we've got two days to enjoy it first."

Junior guard Kyle Guy said he's "like a kid in a candy store this week. This is the stuff we dream of, but at the end of the day I'm just trying to soak it all up, have fun with it but also be as laser-focused as possible."

For UVA assistant coach Brad Soderberg, this is his second Final Four. His first was with Wisconsin in 2000, when he was one of Dick Bennett's assistants. Soderberg's boss at Virginia is Tony Bennett, Dick's son, who was a volunteer manager for the Badgers in 2000.

Soderberg knows well how the hoopla of a Final Four can distract a team.

"The most important thing that we have to understand is it's about Saturday's game, [not] the police escorts and the media things and the video stuff and ESPN," Soderberg said. "It's about the game. And the team that can best understand that at 5 o'clock is going to have a leg up on the other."

In Jerome, Guy, Jack Salt and De'Andre Hunter, the Wahoos have veteran players who should be able to block out all the distractions. Still, Soderberg said, it will be impossible to know for sure until the game starts Saturday night.

"It's an experience that, as prepared as you might think they are, they've never had anything like this," Soderberg said. "It's just crazy."

Bennett's message to his players?

"He tells us to enjoy it but also remain humble and not to let it get to your head," junior forward Braxton Key said. "Honestly, it's a blessing to be here. We were on the other end of it last year."

Starting at noon Central, the 'Hoos will practice for 50 minutes at U.S. Bank Stadium in a session that's open to the public. The stands were empty Thursday morning when the 'Hoos took the court for a practice that was as intense as if they were back at John Paul Jones Arena.

"Everyone was super locked-in," Jerome said, "because we know what we're here for."

Key said: "For a second I forgot I was here, honestly. I forgot I was in Minnesota or how big this arena is. You realize it's just basketball at the end of the day."

Right: Braxton Key signs autographs during Virginia's open practice session.

Matt Riley

Scenes from the days leading up to the Final Four at US Bank Stadium in Minneapolis.

Matt Riley

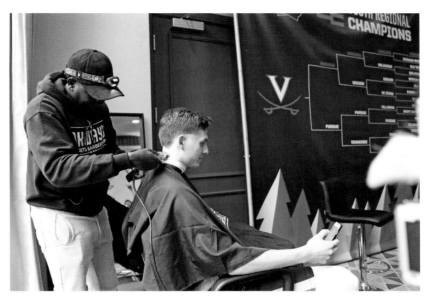

The Cavaliers were all business when they arrived, but still made time to take in the event hoopla, interact with fans at the team hotel and even catch up on homework.

Matt Riley

Never-Say-Die 'Hoos Deliver Again

By Jeff White

April 6, 2019

MINNEAPOLIS — Until Saturday night, the final seconds of regulation against Purdue in last weekend's Elite Eight constituted perhaps the most unforgettable sequence in the history of University of Virginia men's basketball. Who knew that was a mere prelude to more heart-stopping drama at the Final Four?

Junior guard Kyle Guy scored six points in the final 7.4 seconds – the final three coming on free throws with six-tenths of a second left – to send the Cavaliers to the NCAA championship game for the first time.

UVA 63, Auburn 62.

"I could lie to you and say I knew I was going to hit them, but I was terrified," Guy said.

Maybe so, but he couldn't have looked more composed at the line. Each free throw dropped through the net, and the Wahoos moved on.

Virginia (34-3) will meet Texas Tech (31-6), which ousted Michigan State in the second semifinal, for the NCAA title at U.S. Bank Stadium.

"We found a way," associate head coach Jason Williford said. "I don't know what else to say. I'm at a loss for words."

He wasn't the only one who felt that way. For much of the second half, the 'Hoos were in control of their first NCAA semifinal in 35 years, and junior guard Ty Jerome's 3-pointer pushed their lead to 57-47 with 5:19 to play.

But Virginia began to sputter at both ends of the court, and the Tigers (30-10) responded with 14 straight points, the last two in that run coming on free throws by Anfernee McLemore with 17.6 seconds to play.

As was the case last weekend in the South Region final against Purdue, UVA's season was in peril. Again, the 'Hoos pressed on.

With 7.4 seconds left, Guy's contested 3-pointer from the right corner cut Auburn's lead to 61-60. The Cavaliers then fouled guard Jared Harper, sending him to the line for a one-and-one. Harper made the front end but missed his second foul shot, and Jerome rebounded.

The Tigers had two fouls to give before Virginia began shooting the bonus, and they used the first with 5.4 seconds left. Auburn fouled again with 1.5 seconds remaining, after which UVA head coach Tony Bennett called a timeout to set up a last-second shot for Guy.

"It's a play we put in and practiced it multiple times," Jerome said. "It wasn't just luck. We worked on that situation a lot."

Inbounding the ball from the left sideline, Jerome passed to Guy in the left corner. Guy rose for a 3-point attempt that Auburn's Samir Doughty contested. The shot missed, and the Tigers began to celebrate, only to realize that official James Breeding had called a foul on Doughty.

Breeding ruled that Doughty had moved into an airborne shooter, making contact with Guy while taking away his landing spot.

The foul was a violation of Rule 4, Second 39.i., national coordinator of officiating J.D. Collins explained in a statement released after the game.

Right: Kyle Guy sinks the foul shot to put Virginia in the national title game.

Associated Press

∞∞

'This is what we work for our whole life as kids growing up in the gym.'

Kihei Clark

"This will be a memorable game, and I'd like it to be remembered for [being] a great game," Auburn head coach Bruce Pearl said when asked about the call. "Let's not remember this game because of just how it ended."

Guy, of course, still had to make the free throws, and the 'Hoos were 3 for 9 from the line at that point.

"I was saying that to [assistant coach Orlando Vandross] on the bench, 'We haven't made our free throws tonight,' " Williford said. "But give Kyle credit. He stepped up and banged 'em."

Redshirt junior Mamadi Diakite's assessment? "He was cold-blooded."

With the other four Cavaliers watching from near midcourt, Guy calmly made his first two foul shots. Pearl called a timeout before the third, but that didn't faze Guy, who triggered jubilation among the UVA fans in the crowd of 72,711 with his 15th and final point.

"I just literally told myself that we dream of these moments, and to be able to make one happen was special," Guy said.

Bennett said: "We struggled from the line, but for him in that setting to do it, it doesn't get much better than that."

And so another chapter was added to the remarkable story the Cavaliers have been writing all season. A year after falling to UMBC in the NCAA tournament's first round, thus becoming the first No. 1 seed ever to lose to a No. 16 seed, UVA will play for a national title.

"It's crazy," said redshirt sophomore forward De'Andre Hunter, who scored 10 of his 14 points in the second half and also finished with five rebounds, two assists and two blocked shots.

"Especially after a game like that coming down to the last moments, it's a blessing to be in the championship."

Jerome led the Cavaliers in points (21), rebounds (nine) and assists (six).

"I feel like I get asked this question every single round, every round we advance, and every round I say the same thing almost, and it feels a little bit sweeter, a little bit sweeter," Jerome said.

"But to think this time last year we were starting our spring workouts, and to still be playing at this point in the season with, after tonight, one other team in the whole country on the stage that you dreamed about since you were a little kid, it's an unreal feeling. We're going to do everything we can to finish the job."

Two years ago, Florida blew out UVA in the NCAA tournament's second round. One year ago, UMBC humbled Virginia.

Guy and Jerome experienced both of those defeats, and "now to sit with them here brings great joy to my heart, it really does, because it's good," Bennett said at the postgame press conference. "That's all I can say, and I'm so thankful."

Each of Virginia's starters played at least 34 minutes against Auburn. The 6-9 Diakite scored only two points but had six rebounds and a career-best five blocks. Freshman point guard Kihei Clark contributed nine points, three assists, one steal and no turnovers.

"It's crazy," Clark said. "This is what we work for our whole life as kids growing up in the gym, working out. It's truly a blessing."

Kyle Guy is fouled by Auburn's Samir Doughty as he attempts a three-pointer in the final seconds of the Final Four matchup. Guy sank three free throws to put the 'Hoos in the national championship game.

Associated Press

Kihei Clark drives to the basket against Auburn. Clark scored 9 points in the game.

Matt Riley

Ty Jerome pulls up for a jump shot against Auburn in the Final Four in Minneapolis.

Matt Riley

De'Andre Hunter scores two more against Auburn.

Matt Riley

UNITED PURSUIT

Coach Tony Bennett meets with his team in the locker room after the win over Auburn.

Matt Riley

Scenes from
the stands and
sidelines during
Virginia's
thrilling Final
Four victory
over Auburn.

Matt Riley

MOONEY
PTS REB STL BLK AST
2019 NCAA FINAL FOUR
THE ROAD ENDS HERE
VIRGINIA
2019 NCAA FINAL FOUR
VIRGINIA
TEXAS TECH
MINNEAPOLIS
NCAA FINAL FOUR
FINAL FOUR
THE ROAD ENDS HERE

Virginia and Texas Tech tip off in the national championship game.

Associated Press

National Champions!

By Jeff White

April 8, 2019

MINNEAPOLIS — In the stands at U.S. Bank Stadium, as the final seconds ticked off the clock in overtime, Joe Harris reflected on another night, one that came much earlier in Tony Bennett's tenure as the University of Virginia's head men's basketball coach.

Long before the Cavaliers established themselves as national powers, they were in Durham, N.C., to play mighty Duke. During a shootaround at Cameron Indoor Stadium the night before a game in 2011, the players were on the court when they noticed Bennett was no longer with them.

Then they heard him calling to them. They looked up and saw Bennett high in the stands at Cameron, jumping up and down and pointing to Duke's NCAA championship banners.

"He said, 'This is what we're reaching for,'" said Harris, who's now with the Brooklyn Nets.

Harris smiled. "And we did it."

The moment toward which the Cavaliers had been building in their 10 seasons under Bennett arrived. Before a crowd of 72,062 and a national television audience, UVA defeated Texas Tech 85-77 in overtime to capture the first NCAA title in program history.

In his office at John Paul Jones Arena, Bennett has a poster from the film *Rocky* that shows the title character on the steps of the Philadelphia Museum of Art. Bennett would tell his players, he said, that he just wanted a chance at a title fight one day.

"That's all we want," Bennett said, "and these guys came to fight in this title [bout], and now we are the champs."

The championship came about 13 months after the Wahoos made a different kind of history in last year's NCAA tournament. Virginia became the first No. 1 seed ever to lose to a No. 16 seed, falling to UMBC in Charlotte, N.C.

"It's a great story," Bennett said at his postgame press conference. "That's probably the best way I can end this. It's a great story."

Without the contributions of 6-9 redshirt junior Mamadi Diakite, who had nine points and seven rebounds, and 6-8 junior Braxton Key, who came off the bench to score six points and grab a game-high 10 rebounds, the Cavaliers (35-3) might not have won.

But it's impossible to overstate the impact of UVA's Big Three: 6-5 junior Ty Jerome, 6-2 junior Kyle Guy and 6-7 redshirt sophomore De'Andre Hunter.

Jerome totaled 16 points, eight assists, six rebounds and only one turnover, and Guy scored 24 points and was named Most Outstanding Player of the Final Four.

That award could have gone to Hunter, who enrolled at UVA with Guy and Jerome in 2016. After a first half in which he missed 7 of 8 shots from the floor, Hunter turned in one of the most memorable performances in UVA history.

"He saved his best for last," Bennett said.

Hunter finished with a career-high 27 points and also had 9 rebounds. Equally important, he helped limit Texas Tech's Jarrett Culver, who like Hunter is a projected first-round NBA draft pick, into a miserable outing. Culver scored 15 points but was only 5 of 22 from the floor.

"He's a great player," Culver said of Hunter. "Athletic. He played me well tonight."

Hunter said: "I dreamed of this as a kid, just having a great game on the biggest stage in college basketball." ∞

**Right:
The 'Hoos
celebrate
after beating
Texas Tech for
the national
championship.**
Matt Riley

'Words aren't very accurate when your emotions overrun them, and that's kind of where I am right now'

Dick Bennett, father of Virginia coach Tony Bennett, after the national championship

He was 4 for 5 from beyond the 3-point arc, and two of those treys rank among the most pivotal in Final Four history.

On the first, Hunter took a pass from Jerome and buried a 3-pointer from the right corner to tie the game at 68-68 with 12.9 seconds left in regulation.

The second, again off a Jerome assist, put UVA ahead for good, 75-73, with 2:06 in overtime. That was part of the 11-0 run with which the 'Hoos seized command in the extra period.

"He's a quiet kid," associate head coach Jason Williford said of Hunter, a Philadelphia native. "He doesn't have that New York swag that Ty's got, but he's got a quiet confidence. I couldn't be prouder of the kid. I told him that after the game. That's how you step up."

The championship game matched two of the nation's premier defensive teams. UVA held Texas Tech (31-7) without a field goal for nearly eight minutes to start the game. But the Red Raiders heated up from beyond the arc, and Virginia's lead was only three at halftime.

Midway through the second half, the Cavaliers led 53-43, and a one-sided victory seemed possible. Texas Tech refused to cooperate. The Red Raiders rallied to tie the game at 59-59 with 3:28 to play and took their first lead of the second half on a Culver layup with 35.1 seconds left.

That put Texas Tech up 66-65, and after Jerome missed a runner, Norense Odiase hit two free throws to make it 68-65 with 22.5 seconds remaining. Once again, the Cavaliers were in peril. Once again, they fought back. Once again, they prevailed.

In overtime, the Hoos were 12 for 12 from the line.

"The game was everything we thought it would be," Texas Tech head coach Chris Beard said. "I thought it would come down to one last possession, and it did in regulation, and then in overtime it just got away from us a little bit. Nothing but respect for [the Cavaliers'] program, their coaches, their players, their fans. I thought it was a great national championship game."

It was a game the UVA basketball family will never forget.

Former players such as Harris, Malcolm Brogdon, Devon Hall and Justin Anderson beamed with pride and mingled with the current Cavaliers. In the stands stood many other UVA basketball alumni, including legends Barry Parkhill and Ralph Sampson, as well as several players Bennett coached at Wash-ington State before coming to Charlottesville in 2009.

"This is surreal," said Anderson, who now plays for the Atlanta Hawks.

On the court, Bennett savored the title with his wife and their children, as well as his mother, Anne, and his father, Dick, the legendary former coach whom Tony succeeded at Washington State.

Dick Bennett, who guided Wisconsin to the Final Four in 2000 – his son was a volunteer manager on that team -- nervously followed the championship game as it unfolded.

"Words aren't very accurate when your emotions outrun them, and that's kind of where I am right now," the elder Bennett said.

Not far away were UVA's president, Jim Ryan, and athletic director, Carla Williams, as well as Williams' predecessor as AD, Craig Littlepage, who hired Tony Bennett back in 2009. Also in the joyous throng were such notable UVA alumni as Chris Long, Tiki Barber and Katie Couric. ∞

Braxton Key's crucial block on Texas Tech's Jarrett Culver late in regulation.

Associated Press

'I've watched every single One Shining Moment, every single one. And we watched it last year, and last year it [showed] Kyle and me walking off the court after the UMBC game, Kyle with his head down, and I put my hand on his head. So, this year, to watch it like that was unbelievable.'

Ty Jerome

After Bennett cut down the final strand of the net, the Cavaliers returned to the platform on which they'd received the NCAA championship trophy and turned their attention to the videoboard. They watched, transfixed, as the traditional finale to the NCAA tournament – CBS' One Shining Moment video – played.

"I've watched every single One Shining Moment, every single one," Jerome said. "And we watched it last year, and last year it [showed] Kyle and me walking off the court after the UMBC game, Kyle with his head down, and I put my hand on his head. So, this year, to watch it like that was unbelievable."

Little came easily in this NCAA tournament for Virginia (35-3), the only No. 1 seed to reach the Final Four. In the Cavaliers' first-round game, they trailed No. 16 seed Gardner-Webb by 14 points in the first half before rallying for a 71-56 win.

There was less suspense in the 'Hoos' second-round win over Oklahoma, but they had to rally late to defeat Oregon in the Sweet Sixteen, and their next two games produced almost indescribable drama.

In the Elite Eight, UVa needed a miraculous sequence at the end of regulation to force overtime against Purdue. Then, in the first NCAA semifinal Saturday night, junior guard Kyle Guy scored six points in the final 7.4 seconds – the final three coming on free throws with six-tenths of a second left – to lift Virginia past Auburn and into its first NCAA championship game.

"I think we've taken every experience that we've been through together and tried to use it in a way that could propel us to a national championship," Guy said.

"I never thought of myself being a national championship coach," Bennett said. "I wasn't even going to really get into coaching. I wasn't crazy about it. I loved playing, and then I saw my dad's team go to the Final Four. I was a volunteer manager, and I got into it. I love the young men. I love the game. But it's not my end all, be all.

"I think there was a bigger plan going on here, and I didn't need it, but I was used in it. I hope that it's a message for some people out there that there can be hope and joy and resiliency. I'm thankful for what happened. That's why I did what I did at the end. When that horn went off, I just put my head down and said,

'Thank you. I'm humbled, Lord, because I don't deserve to be in this spot, but You chose me to be here, and I'll give thanks.'"

The championship, said Williford, who played for the Cavaliers in the 1990s, is "for everybody, from Parkhill to Ralph to my crew [and the teams that came after]. And then you got all the guys we coached.

"It's for all of those basketball alums. It's for all the alumni. It's for everybody. It's a great day to be a Wahoo."

Williford took over as associate head coach last spring after Ron Sanchez left UVA to become head coach at Charlotte. Sanchez flew to Minneapolis for the Final Four to support his former team and his mentor, Bennett. Sanchez also worked for Bennett at Washington State, as did Ronnie Wideman, Virginia's associate AD for men's basketball.

"Can you believe this?" Wideman asked Sanchez as they wrapped each other in a bear hug.

Believe it.

Right: Ty Jerome hits a clutch turnaround jump shot late in the second half against Texas Tech.

Associated Press

Right: Before, during and after the 'Hoos defeated Texas Tech, 85-77, in overtime to claim the 2019 national championship at US Bank Stadium in Minneapolis. Far right: De'Andre Hunter drains a crucial 3-pointer late in regulation to tie the game against Texas Tech.

Matt Riley

Braxton Key dunks against Texas Tech in the national championship game.

Associated Press

The confetti falls as the Cavaliers celebrate a national championship.

Associated Press

MICHIGAN STATE

VIRGINIA
NATIONAL CHAMPION

TEXAS TECH

2019
FINAL
FOUR

MINNEAPOLIS

VIRGINIA

TEXAS TECH

The postgame celebration for the 2019 national champions.

Matt Riley

Kyle Guy, De'Andre Hunter and Ty Jerome celebrate winning the national championship.

Matt Riley

'Hoos Bask in Glow of Championship

By Jeff White

April 9, 2019

MINNEAPOLIS — For nearly a week, the Marquette Hotel served as home base for University of Virginia men's basketball team during the Final Four. The Cavaliers ate, slept, watched film, and visited with their families there.

Mamadi Diakite was the first player down for breakfast Tuesday at the Marquette. He hadn't slept much, but his mood was upbeat.

"I can't stop smiling," Diakite said.

Who could blame him? About 10 hours earlier, the Cavaliers had reached the summit of their sport, defeating Texas Tech 85-77 in overtime to secure the first NCAA title in program history.

A 6-9 redshirt junior from Guinea, Diakite scored nine points and grabbed seven rebounds.

Other standouts for the Wahoos included junior forward Braxton Key, who pulled down a game-high 10 rebounds, and the three players who have led the team all season: junior guards Ty Jerome and Kyle Guy and redshirt sophomore forward De'Andre Hunter.

"To share it with this special group of guys is unreal," Jerome said late Monday night at U.S. Bank Stadium.

"I'll remember it for the rest of my life," Hunter said.

Hunter, who played superb defense on Texas Tech star Jarrett Culver, scored 22 of his career-high 27 points after intermission to lead Virginia (35-3).

"He's an amazing player, but beyond that, he's an amazing person, and he deserves whatever he gets with his basketball [career]," Virginia center Jack Salt, a fifth-year senior, said of Hunter.

The 'Hoos' flight home to Charlottesville on Tuesday afternoon was bumpy at times, which was perhaps fitting for a team that encountered significant obstacles in its NCAA tournament journey.

None proved to be insurmountable. These Cavaliers were as mentally tough as they were talented.

On Monday night, a crowd of 72,062 at U.S. Bank Stadium saw Virginia rally late in the second half for the third straight game. Two of those games – UVA's wins over Purdue in the Elite Eight and Texas Tech in the final – went to overtime. In the other, Guy scored six points in the final 7.4 seconds to lift Virginia past Auburn in the semifinals.

"We just play until that buzzer sounds," Jerome said. "We all believe in each other, and it's the most special team I've ever been on."

Hunter: "It's crazy. We were destined to win."

In a story Hollywood could have scripted, the Cavaliers' calamitous 2017-18 finale forged the bond that united them this season in their pursuit of a championship. In the first round of last year's NCAA tournament, UVA became the first No. 1 seed ever to lose to a No. 16 seed, falling to UMBC in Charlotte, N.C.

"It was humiliation, embarrassment for ourselves and our families and the program," said Guy, who was named the Final Four's Most Outstanding Player. "To be able to redeem all that and get this program something that's never happened before is all that I could ever want."

The UMBC loss "drew us even closer together, and it made us enjoy every part of [this] season even more, and made us enjoy each other's company more on the road," Jerome said. "We grew closer together off the court.'"

Right: Ty Jerome has no plans to let go of the trophy after winning UVA's first national title.

Matt Riley

∞∞∞

'I guess this really happened. I guess we won the national championship.'

Coach Tony Bennett

Overseeing it all, of course, was Tony Bennett, who's built a national power in his 10 seasons as the Cavaliers' head coach. The win over Texas Tech improved Bennett's record at UVA to 254-89, with seven trips to the NCAA tournament.

For the past four seasons, his assistants have included Brad Soderberg, who played for Bennett's father, Dick, at Wisconsin-Stevens Point and later coached under the elder Bennett at Wisconsin.

Soderberg has been a head coach at several schools, including Saint Louis. He said he was confident Tony Bennett would eventually break through and win an NCAA title.

"You can't guarantee anything in this business, but he is elite," Soderberg said in UVA's locker room after the championship game. "If you make a list of the 10 things every coach has to have to some degree – [for example] they've got to be recruiters, they have to have an on-court disposition, they have to have great Xs and Os knowledge, they have to have a story to tell – Tony is A-plus, A-plus, A-plus, A-plus.

"I know I'm a Bennett myself, basically, so it's a biased opinion. But I'm not joking. I've been around a long time. I've worked with a lot of guys. I haven't been with a guy like this.

His knowledge of the game, his interaction with players is real and genuine. His disposition on the bench is uncanny. His poise under pressure is unbelievable. You just don't find that."

The loss to UMBC, Bennett has acknowledged, hurt him deeply. But it didn't change his values, he said after the final.

"You have a scar, and it reminds you of that, but it's a memory," Bennett said. "Does it go away completely? No. I wish it wouldn't have happened in some ways. Now I say, well, it bought us a ticket here. So be it.

"I'm thankful in a way for what happened because it did, it drew me closer, most importantly, to my faith in the Lord, drew me closer to my wife and children, just because you realize what's unconditional. In those spots when the world's telling you you're a failure, you're a loser, and you're the worst thing going, and all that stuff, you say, OK, what really matters? And it pushed me to that in a way.

"Then it drove me. I think as a staff we became better. We had to look at how can we change if we're in this spot again and we play certain teams, and we adjusted to things. Again, that helped, all the lessons from that."

For Bennett's players, Guy said, to "be able to give him a national championship and do it for him, the program, and our families, it means the world, and I wish I had the words, but it still does not feel real."

If the NCAA title is a milestone the Cavaliers will savor forever, their homecoming Tuesday was special too. Fans were waiting at Charlottesville Albemarle Airport when UVA's charter flight landed, and they cheered the players and coaches as the team disembarked.

With a police escort, the 'Hoos then bused to John Paul Jones Arena.

On both sides of Airport Road and Route 29 stood fans who waved and cheered as the buses passed.

That was a prelude for what awaited the Cavaliers at JPJ, where thousands of jubilant fans welcomed the team home. Guy addressed the crowd briefly, as did Bennett.

"I guess this really happened. I guess we won the national championship," Bennett said, to loud cheers. "What these guys did under the bright lights was amazing. I just felt like I was going along for the ride."

Top and left: The nets come down after the 'Hoos beat Texas Tech.

Matt Riley

Bottom right: Tony Bennett with his dad, Dick Bennett, after the game.

Jim Daves

Exultant Crowd Salutes NCAA Champions

By Jeff White

April 13, 2019

CHARLOTTESVILLE — John Paul Jones Arena was not available for the championship celebration Saturday afternoon. Even if it had been, Virginia coach Tony Bennett was told, the 14,623-seat arena couldn't have handled all the fans who wanted to pay tribute to his basketball team.

Bennett was skeptical. "I was like, 'Come on,'" he said.

At about 2:25 p.m. Saturday, his thinking changed. Bennett emerged from the home locker room at Scott Stadium, saw the multitudes in the stands, and was reminded that it's a mistake to underestimate the ardor of fans for these Cavaliers.

A crowd of 21,000, many of whose members had entered the stadium at 12:30 p.m., was waiting for the Wahoos, who on Monday night had capped their 10th season under Bennett with an overtime victory over Texas Tech in the NCAA champion-ship game in Minneapolis.

"I'm in awe of this," Bennett told the crowd. "This is more than I ever expected, so thank you for being here. This is a great day to celebrate."

It was a day for which UVA fans have been waiting for decades. Before this season, the 'Hoos had advanced to the Final Four twice – in 1981 and '84 – but each time they lost in the semifinals.

In 2018, Virginia entered the NCAA tournament as the No. 1 overall seed, only to make history by losing to No. 16 seed UMBC in the first round.

"To be back a year later and be here is the best story in college basketball history," former UVA great Ralph Sampson told the crowd at Scott Stadium.

Virginia, which shared the ACC's regular-season title, entered this NCAA tournament as the South Region's No. 1 seed. This year, there were no hurdles the Cavaliers couldn't clear in the NCAA tournament.

His team, Bennett said, was "strengthened by the blow that cut us down last year."

Even so, little came easily for the 'Hoos in the postseason. In the NCAA tournament, they needed memorable comebacks to get past Gardner-Webb, Purdue, Auburn and Texas Tech. Moreover, in the Cavaliers' Sweet Sixteen victory over Oregon, they trailed late in the second half.

"They're part of one of the greatest stories that I've ever seen written, and it'll be told over and over again," Bennett said.

∞∞∞

Ty Jerome greets Cavalier fans at a campus celebration at Scott Stadium.

Matt Riley

'They're part of one of the greatest stories that I've ever seen written, and it'll be told over and over again.'

Coach Tony Bennett

"I'm kind of at a loss for words for what we accomplished," junior guard Kyle Guy said.

The Cavaliers' theme all season has been United Pursuit, and Bennett saw a "united celebration" at the stadium Saturday.

"This community has been through a lot," Bennett said. "[UVA's championship run] is healing in so many ways, and that was not lost on any of us."

During the regular season, the Cavaliers went 18-2 away from John Paul Jones Arena. One of those victories came Jan. 12 at Littlejohn Coliseum, where Virginia defeated Clemson 63-43.

On its way to the arena that morning, UVA's team bus passed Clemson Memorial Stadium, where tens of thousands of fans had turned out to celebrate the school's national title in football.

"I remember thinking, 'Man, what would that be like if we ever won a national championship?' And you know what? That day is now!" Bennett told the crowd at Scott Stadium, to deafening applause.

Throughout the celebration, highlights played on the HooVision videoboard, allowing fans to relive some of the countless memorable moments from this historic season, including Clark's assist on Diakite's buzzer-beater against Purdue, Guy's late 3-pointer and three free throws against Auburn, and Jerome's pass to Hunter for a game-tying trey against Texas Tech.

"It'll be a memory forever," Bennett said.

Likewise, no one who was at Scott Stadium on Saturday – or watched the celebration online – will soon forget seeing and hearing Francesco Badocchi, a redshirt freshman forward from Italy, play One Shining Moment on the piano placed for him on stage.

Songs played over the PA included two whose messages resonated with Bennett: Kaleena Zanders' Stronger Than I've Ever Been and Andy Grammer's Back Home.

As the fans filed out of the stadium, Guy and Bennett held a brief press conference in Scott Stadium's media room.

Bennett asked about the size of the crowd. When told that 21,000 fans had attended, he and Guy marveled at the figure.

"That's insane," Guy said. "It was amazing just to be able to witness that with my coaches and my teammates."

Right: It was a good thing John Paul Jones Arena was already in use when the 'Hoos held a national championship celebration in Charlottesville, because there would not have been room for all the fans who showed up. The party moved to Scott Stadium, where more than 21,000 students, alumni and community members celebrated the school's first national title. *Matt Riley*

A United Pursuit to Remember Forever

Ten years ago, I came to the University of Virginia to build a program that lasts. I came because UVA is a place where I believed we could have it all: high-level basketball in the best conference in the country, elite academic experiences for our students, and a unique connection with a supportive community. The culmination of this journey occurred on a Monday night in Minneapolis.

The way our fans have embraced this program over the last decade is remarkable. It has allowed us to make John Paul Jones Arena one of the most difficult places to play in the country. JPJ gets loud when the shot clock winds down, and our fans celebrate shot clock violations and defensive stops. This doesn't happen everywhere.

We built our program on five pillars: humility, passion, unity, servanthood and thankfulness. Our program's system and values have been accepted and integrated into the fabric of the university community. This was never more evident than in the aftermath of the unexpected end to our 2017-18 season in the first round of the NCAA Tournament.

That devastating loss to UMBC became the foundation for our championship season in 2019. It brought our team closer together, forced our coaches to evolve, and made us all value the importance of relying on each other.

With that understanding, our theme became a "United Pursuit" to ensure that we would stay connected with each other through each workout, meeting, film session, practice and game. We were tested throughout the year, but our players remained united to each other and faithful to our program's pillars and identity.

I truly wanted our players to have the chance at a title fight on the national stage. The resiliency and togetherness they showed throughout this year's NCAA tournament is the lasting memory that I will have of this group. Each step during the journey required a different player to shine in order for us to advance. I am thankful for every player that has worn the Virginia jersey, along with our coaches, managers and support staff. I am also thankful for our faithful fans who have supported us every step of the way. This was a United Pursuit we all will never forget.

Go 'Hoos!

— **Tony Bennett**

Season Statistics

15.4

Points per game for top scorer Kyle Guy.

5.3

Rebounds per game for top rebounder Braxton Key.

5.5

Assists per game for Ty Jerome, which led the team.

Right: Braxton Key, leading rebounder.

Matt Riley

		MINUTES				TOTAL			3-POINTERS			FREE THROWS			REBOUNDS								SCORING		
		GP	GS	Tot	Avg	FG	FGA	Pct	3FG	FGA	Pct	FT	FTA	Pct	Off	Def	Tot	Avg	PF	FO	A	TO	Blk	Stl	Pts	Avg
05	Kyle Guy	38	38	1344	35.4	198	441	.449	120	282	.426	70	84	.833	27	144	171	4.5	39	0	78	53	2	26	586	15.4
12	De'Andre Hunter	38	38	1234	32.5	205	394	.520	46	105	.438	123	157	.783	52	141	193	5.1	76	3	75	52	22	22	579	15.2
11	Ty Jerome	37	37	1256	33.9	178	409	.435	79	198	.399	67	91	.736	17	139	156	4.2	64	0	202	61	1	57	502	13.6
25	Mamadi Diakite	38	22	829	21.8	121	220	.550	5	17	.294	35	50	.700	56	112	168	4.4	81	0	12	34	63	17	282	7.4
02	Braxton Key	38	6	753	19.8	74	171	.433	18	59	.305	49	67	.731	50	150	200	5.3	66	0	38	28	21	36	215	5.7
00	Kihei Clark	38	20	1018	26.8	55	157	.350	29	85	.341	33	40	.825	16	73	89	2.3	52	0	97	39	0	28	172	4.5
30	Jay Huff	34	0	318	9.4	58	96	.604	14	31	.452	20	30	.667	19	54	73	2.1	50	0	8	17	25	8	150	4.4
33	Jack Salt	37	29	614	16.6	56	93	.602	0	0	.000	24	47	.511	55	83	138	3.7	80	1	16	24	11	12	136	3.7
23	Kody Stattmann	18	0	73	4.1	9	21	.429	4	15	.267	8	9	.889	2	9	11	0.6	8	0	2	5	0	1	30	1.7
01	Grant Kersey	10	0	17	1.7	3	3	1.000	2	2	1.000	5	5	1.000	1	1	2	0.2	0	0	1	2	0	2	13	1.3
24	Marco Anthony	22	0	119	5.4	8	27	.296	2	7	.286	8	12	.667	0	12	12	0.5	10	0	11	8	1	0	26	1.2
45	Austin Katstra	11	0	29	2.6	4	10	.400	2	8	.250	0	0	.000	1	5	6	0.5	4	0	3	1	1	0	10	0.9
10	Jayden Nixon	14	0	43	3.1	3	10	.300	0	3	.000	2	4	.500	3	5	8	0.6	10	0	1	4	2	2	8	0.6
01	Francesco Badocchi	11	0	28	2.5	2	4	.500	0	1	.000	1	2	.500	3	3	6	0.5	2	0	0	0	0	0	5	0.5
	Team														46	43	89					14				
	Total	38		7675		974	2056	.474	321	813	.395	445	598	.744	348	974	1322	34.8	542	4	544	342	149	211	2714	71.4
	Opponents......	38		7679		769	1995	.385	245	848	.289	349	524	.666	331	798	1129	29.7	592	-	333	404	103	189	2132	56.1

Game-by-Game Results

35-3
Overall.

16-2
ACC.

15-1
Home.

10-1
Away.

10-1
Neutral.

G	Date		Opp					OT	W	L	Streak	Arena
1	Tue, Nov 6, 2018		Towson	CAA	W	73	42		1	0	W 1	John Paul Jones Arena
2	Sun, Nov 11, 2018		George Washington	A-10	W	76	57		2	0	W 2	John Paul Jones Arena
3	Fri, Nov 16, 2018		Coppin State	MEAC	W	97	40		3	0	W 3	John Paul Jones Arena
4	Wed, Nov 21, 2018	N	Middle Tennessee	CUSA	W	74	52		4	0	W 4	Imperial Arena at Atlantis Resort
5	Thu, Nov 22, 2018	N	Dayton	A-10	W	66	59		5	0	W 5	Imperial Arena at Atlantis Resort
6	Fri, Nov 23, 2018	N	Wisconsin (25)	Big Ten	W	53	46		6	0	W 6	Imperial Arena at Atlantis Resort
7	Wed, Nov 28, 2018	@	Maryland (24)	Big Ten	W	76	71		7	0	W 7	Xfinity Center
8	Mon, Dec 3, 2018		Morgan State	MEAC	W	83	45		8	0	W 8	John Paul Jones Arena
9	Sun, Dec 9, 2018		Virginia Commonwealth	A-10	W	57	49		9	0	W 9	John Paul Jones Arena
10	Wed, Dec 19, 2018	@	South Carolina	SEC	W	69	52		10	0	W 10	Colonial Life Arena
11	Sat, Dec 22, 2018		William & Mary	CAA	W	72	40		11	0	W 11	John Paul Jones Arena
12	Mon, Dec 31, 2018		Marshall	CUSA	W	100	64		12	0	W 12	John Paul Jones Arena
13	Sat, Jan 5, 2019		Florida State (9)	ACC	W	65	52		13	0	W 13	John Paul Jones Arena
14	Wed, Jan 9, 2019	@	Boston College	ACC	W	83	56		14	0	W 14	Silvio O. Conte Forum
15	Sat, Jan 12, 2019	@	Clemson	ACC	W	63	43		15	0	W 15	Littlejohn Coliseum
16	Tue, Jan 15, 2019		Virginia Tech (9)	ACC	W	81	59		16	0	W 16	John Paul Jones Arena
17	Sat, Jan 19, 2019	@	Duke (1)	ACC	L	70	72		16	1	L 1	Cameron Indoor Stadium
18	Tue, Jan 22, 2019		Wake Forest	ACC	W	68	45		17	1	W 1	John Paul Jones Arena
19	Sat, Jan 26, 2019	@	Notre Dame	ACC	W	82	55		18	1	W 2	Purcell Pavilion at the Joyce Center
20	Tue, Jan 29, 2019	@	North Carolina State (23)	ACC	W	66	65	OT	19	1	W 3	PNC Arena
21	Sat, Feb 2, 2019		Miami (FL)	ACC	W	56	46		20	1	W 4	John Paul Jones Arena
22	Sat, Feb 9, 2019		Duke (2)	ACC	L	71	81		20	2	L 1	John Paul Jones Arena
23	Mon, Feb 11, 2019	@	North Carolina (8)	ACC	W	69	61		21	2	W 1	Dean Smith Center
24	Sat, Feb 16, 2019		Notre Dame	ACC	W	60	54		22	2	W 2	John Paul Jones Arena
25	Mon, Feb 18, 2019	@	Virginia Tech (20)	ACC	W	64	58		23	2	W 3	Cassell Coliseum
26	Sat, Feb 23, 2019	@	Louisville (18)	ACC	W	64	52		24	2	W 4	KFC Yum! Center
27	Wed, Feb 27, 2019		Georgia Tech	ACC	W	81	51		25	2	W 5	John Paul Jones Arena
28	Sat, Mar 2, 2019		Pittsburgh	ACC	W	73	49		26	2	W 6	John Paul Jones Arena
29	Mon, Mar 4, 2019	@	Syracuse	ACC	W	79	53		27	2	W 7	Carrier Dome
30	Sat, Mar 9, 2019		Louisville	ACC	W	73	68		28	2	W 8	John Paul Jones Arena
ACC Tournament												
31	Thu, Mar 14, 2019	N	North Carolina State	ACC	W	76	56		29	2	W 9	Spectrum Center
32	Fri, Mar 15, 2019	N	Florida State (12)	ACC	L	59	69		29	3	L 1	Spectrum Center
NCAA Tournament												
33	Fri, Mar 22, 2019	N	Gardner-Webb	Big South	W	71	56		30	3	W 1	Colonial Life Arena
34	Sun, Mar 24, 2019	N	Oklahoma	Big 12	W	63	51		31	3	W 2	Colonial Life Arena
35	Thu, Mar 28, 2019	N	Oregon	Pac-12	W	53	49		32	3	W 3	KFC Yum! Center
36	Sat, Mar 30, 2019	N	Purdue (13)	Big Ten	W	80	75	OT	33	3	W 4	KFC Yum! Center
37	Sat, Apr 6, 2019	N	Auburn (14)	SEC	W	63	62		34	3	W 5	U.S. Bank Stadium
38	Mon, Apr 8, 2019	N	Texas Tech (9)	Big 12	W	85	77	OT	35	3	W 6	U.S. Bank Stadium

Right: A Cavaliers' team photo at the Final Four.

Matt Riley

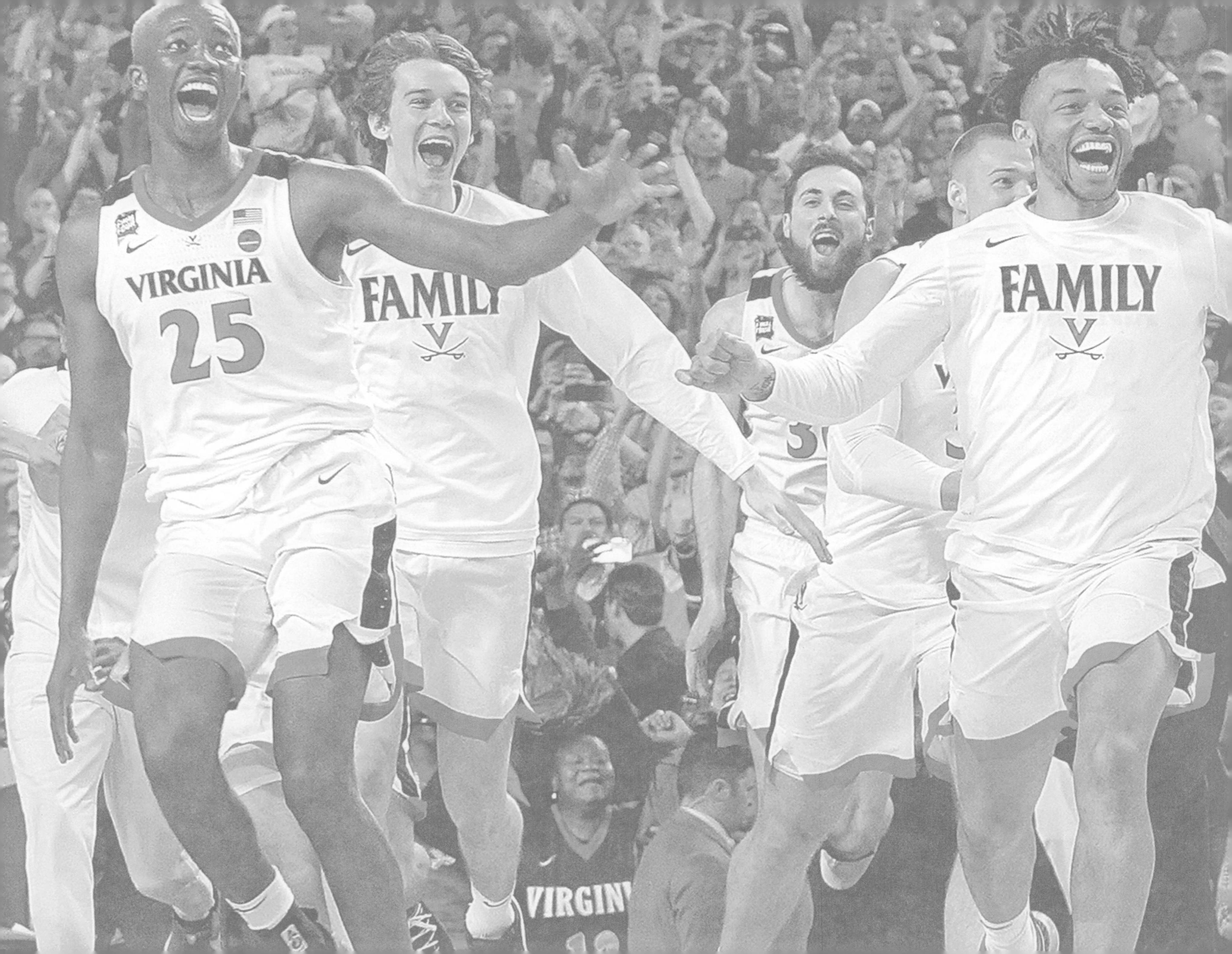
VIRGINIA
25
FAMILY
FAMILY
VIRGINI